Sustainability
in
Australian business

fundamental principles and practice

Geoffrey Wells

WILEY

John Wiley & Sons Australia, Ltd

First published 2011 by
John Wiley & Sons Australia, Ltd
42 McDougall St, Milton Qld 4064

© Geoffrey Wells 2011

ISBN 978 1 74246 500 5

The moral rights of the author have been asserted.

Cover image: © Petoo, 2010 Used under licence from Shutterstock

Printed in China by
Printplus Limited

10 9 8 7 6 5 4 3

Contents

Preface

Business has always operated under an agreement with its society. In part that agreement is codified in corporate legislation and regulation; in part it is situated in community standards and values. For most of its history, the dominant setting for that agreement has been economic. As Peter Drucker has framed it, with customary clarity: 'Economic performance is the specific function and contribution of business enterprise, and the reason for its existence. It is work to obtain economic performance and results' (Drucker 1968, p. xi).

There is no doubting the power of this paradigm of business. In its own terms, it has been enormously successful. The wealth it has generated, and continues to generate, has driven historically unprecedented improvements in the material quality of life throughout the developed world. It stands unambiguously at the centre of all modern economies and societies and of all plans for civil advancement.

In recent decades, however, a perception has grown that the economic paradigm of business is being interpreted and implemented too narrowly. It has been observed that the reach of the modern firm extends outside its defined boundaries: to the environment from which it draws resources and on which its operations impact, and to the wider society — even extending to the global society — with which it is inextricably connected. Accordingly, the terms of the agreement under which business operates have been changing to take systematic account of these wider contexts and impacts. This expanded paradigm of business is being termed 'sustainable business'.

This re-embedding of the firm in the environment and the society of which it is a part requires the firm to change the way it does business. There is a clear economic case for sustainable business, but the demands also reach wider. For example, ethical imperatives become a part of everyday business activities. The sustainable firm considers not just its own part in the value chain of its goods and services, but all segments of that value chain — across the life of its products and across the global economy. It takes account of the people with which it interacts in all its stakeholder groups, including its own people and extending to the community at large. It develops and uses new, sophisticated tools of management, capable of encompassing this increased scale and its associated complexities and volatilities. It sees itself as a steward of resources held in common with present and future generations, and as a primary contributor to the social good.

There is nothing trivial about the transformation of business that the new sustainability paradigm demands. Like all business work, to borrow again from Drucker, sustainable business 'has to be thought through and done with direction, method and purpose'. Where these new ways of thinking about business and new methods of management and implementation are required, however widely, they must be achieved: increasingly it is becoming clear that the firm's stakeholders will accept nothing less. In the view of the author, sustainable business is not a passing fad: it will characterise the firms that become market leaders in this century.

This book is an introduction to the work of thinking through and doing sustainable business. The principles and practices described here are not set in stone: they are emerging and moving every day, as a glance at the daily news will confirm. However, over several decades a body of sustainable business principles and practice has been put in place. The purpose of this book is to present that body of new knowledge in outline. It is offered in the conviction that it is to this knowledge that the stakeholders of business — firms, suppliers, customers, managers, employees, owners, investors, regulators, legislators and communities — will look in framing the business of the sustainability age.

Acknowledgements

I acknowledge the University of South Australia for its contribution to the project. I thank my university colleagues, particularly Professor Helen Thorne and Dr Sukhbir Sandhu, for their support of my pursuit of this new academic frontier. My friend and colleague Dr Lee Fergusson provided important opportunities and support for developing sustainable business as a professional offering. My brothers Dr Sam Wells and Jonathan Wells QC have provided a valuable forum for the discussion of issues in sustainable business and ethics. I am particularly grateful to my graduate students for their collaborative work and support: their insights and enthusiasm have been central to my own intellectual development in this field. Professor Juliet Roper and fellow Board members of the Asia Pacific Academy of Business in Society (APABIS) have provided an environment for stimulating discussion. I acknowledge a long-standing intellectual debt to the late Professor Fay Gale. At John Wiley & Sons, John Coomer and Jacqui Belesky have given exemplary support and advice at every stage of the development of this project.

Dr Geoff Wells
July 2010

Sustainability in Australian business: fundamental principles and practice

Learning objectives

After studying this publication, you should be able to:

1   define the overarching idea of sustainable business

2   describe the historical path of development of sustainability principles and the crystallisation of these principles around a core group of concepts

3   discuss the social context which drives sustainable enterprise, with particular reference to global patterns and the ethical imperatives that derive from them

4   trace the emergence of sustainable business principles in historical accounts of the nature of the firm, and in the foundations of the economics of the firm

5   identify the impacts of sustainability principles on accounting theory and practice, in both financial and management accounting

6   identify the impacts of sustainability factors on financial valuation theory and practice, and its significance for business finance

7   present approaches to reorienting the marketing function to profit from the emergence of the green consumer and of new markets in sustainable goods and services, including the modern discipline of social marketing

8   describe international best practice for operations and production in working with environmental and social regulations and standards

9   present ways of applying sustainability principles to the firm as an organisation, in the domains of governance, change and human resource management.

Introduction

Over recent decades, particularly in developed economies, business has been increasingly subjected to a new kind of public scrutiny. Firms have always been expected to perform in economic terms. Shareholders and investors, and public business commentators, have routinely analysed a firm's competitive advantage and ability to deliver shareholder value; they still do. Beginning in the 1930s, however, and continuing to the present day, debate about the social purpose and impact of firms has been intensifying.

In particular, the idea that firms have a responsibility to the wider social and biophysical environment of which they are a part, from which they draw resources, and to which they contribute has gained ground in public discourse. This responsibility goes beyond the traditional responsibility of the firm to its owners and shareholders to generate economic wealth. This idea seems to demand a re-envisioning of what has been called the 'licence to operate': the implicit social contract by which a society agrees to a firm operating within it, in certain ways, within certain limits and under certain conditions (Institute of Chartered Accountants in England and Wales 1975).

In large part, the emergence of these ideas has been driven by the disclosure and public airing of high-profile events and questions relating to major international companies. The long-term impacts of the Exxon Valdez oil spill in Prince William Sound, Alaska, on the environment and on local communities emerged in over two decades of lawsuits (Carson et al. 2004). The disclosure of Nike's use of sweatshops in developing countries presented a serious challenge to the use of international supply chains in the globalising economy (Maitland 2005). The impact of Shell's oil operations on the environment of the Niger Delta and on the local Ogoni people is still the subject of legal action (Newburry & Gladwin 2002). BHP Billiton's Ok Tedi mine in Papua New Guinea was found in court cases to have delivered pollution into the Fly River that impacted the lives of about 50 000 people, and seriously damaged ecological systems over 1300 square kilometres (Hanson & Stuart 2001). Walmart, a company which has arguably achieved iconic status in the history of US capitalism, continues to face charges of damage to the economies and environments of local communities, and of allegations of serious mistreatment of its own employees (Irwin & Clark 2006). Recent ocean oil spills — in the Timor Sea, on the Great Barrier Reef, and, of course, in the Gulf of Mexico (a spill that is now considered the worst polluting event in US history) — have intensified public discussion about the accountability of firms, the trade-offs associated with regulation, and the underlying patterns of consumption and economic growth.

The questions that have been, and are being, raised around this idea go to the heart of the business enterprise. What are the purposes of the firm? What are its legitimate goals and responsibilities? Who are its stakeholders, and what is owed to them? How should a firm be held accountable by the society of which it is a part, and for what outcomes? Where are the boundaries of a firm? How are a firm's impacts on the wider biophysical and social environment to be effectively handled? It is difficult to think of more fundamental or far-reaching questions about the nature and place of business in modern society. These questions are generating a new approach to business, termed 'sustainable business'.

This introduction to sustainable business is presented in two parts. In Part 1, the core principles of sustainable business, which centre on ways of responding to questions such as those posed, are discussed. Together, these principles provide a coherent framework for a sustainable approach to 'the systematic, purposeful performance of the specific task and function of business enterprise' (Drucker 1968, p. xii).

In Part 2, the framework of sustainable business principles is applied to the core disciplines of business: accounting, finance, marketing, production and organisation. In that task, some current initiatives in the sustainable operation of these disciplines are documented, and further approaches to that task are suggested.

PART 1: SUSTAINABLE BUSINESS PRINCIPLES

What is sustainable business?

Sustainability has become a term of wide currency, yet its definition and scope is far from agreed. There is a general consensus that it seems to cover at least three principal dimensions: the economic, the environmental and the social. Some would want to add governance. Others would want to link it to wellbeing or quality of life, or to the stock of natural and social capital over time.

The application of such principles to business has resulted in what, as noted, is increasingly being termed **sustainable business**. There is an ambiguity here. In one sense of the term, 'sustainable business' can be interpreted simply as 'continuously profitable business' or 'business as a going concern'; and many commentators with an apparent commitment to defending the status quo have taken it in just that way But such a strategy is an intellectual sleight of hand. Certainly that kind of sustainability is a central element of the wider concept: if a business did not survive and grow economically, there would be nothing to talk about. But treating the term 'sustainable' in this way does not begin to capture the full complexity of a firm that is attempting to redefine and transform its business according to widely conceived sustainability principles. In this publication, 'sustainable business' is taken to mean the latter kind of firm. *Sustainable business is the business of firms under sustainability principles.*

So powerful has been this change in the social licence to operate under stronger sustainability principles that nearly all major companies now routinely provide reports of their performance on various sustainability measures. Various indices, such as the Dow Jones Sustainability Index (2007), have been developed to provide comparative public data on sustainability performance. All the companies mentioned have moved to provide sustainability reports, together with accounts of the operational changes implemented to deliver results on those measures. Whether such reports always imply material changes in the way a company operates is open to question, and that question later will be taken up later. For now, the ubiquity of the move to establish sustainability credentials is simply noted. It is a fact of modern business life that the ability of companies, in almost all sectors, to present such credentials credibly has become an important strategic element in the race to build and maintain competitive advantage.

Case study 1

Meeting the sustainable business challenge: Walmart

Walmart is the world's largest retailer, with a market capitalisation of over US$190 billion, and an enterprise value of over US$228 billion. Its more than 7000 stores and supercentres in 14 international markets generate annual revenues of over US$413 billion, with a projected net income of US$14.4 billion (June 2010).

Despite its spectacular expansion and financial success, Walmart has been strongly and widely criticised on a number of corporate social responsibility grounds (Irwin & Clark 2006). In the United States, the company has kept labour costs low by paying its employees less. A Californian study has found that Walmart workers earn almost a third less than industry averages and more than 20 per cent fewer are covered by employer-sponsored health insurance. Walmart faces about 8000 lawsuits from employees at any time, with a large number of class-action lawsuits. It has been the subject of the largest sex discrimination lawsuit, involving some 1.6 million women who are current or former employees.

Local communities have found themselves having to bear significant social costs as Walmart stores were established in their neighbourhoods. Studies have found a positive correlation between Walmart stores and poverty or increased reliance on public assistance programs. In California, Walmart employees have been estimated to use nearly 40 per cent more in public assistance programs than the average for all large-store retail employees. Environmental problems have been associated with large store sites: in 2004 Walmart paid $3.1 million for violating the Clear Water Act with destructive construction practices at 24 stores in nine states.

Despite this controversial record in corporate responsibility, Walmart has now committed itself to ambitious environmental goals in energy, waste and products (Walmart 2010). Walmart will be investing US$500 million annually in technologies and innovation to reduce greenhouse gases in existing stores around the world by 20 per cent over a seven-year period; to design and open within the next few years a store prototype that is 30 per cent more efficient and produces up to 30 per cent fewer greenhouse gas emissions; to reduce solid waste from US stores by 25 per cent in the next few years; to increase its truck fleet efficiency by 25 per cent over the next few years, and to double it within ten years. On the revenue side, Walmart is well aware of the emerging market in clean products, such as solar panels and green building materials, and is coordinating the new business with General Electric. It is establishing Life Cycle Assessment capacity, and an innovative tool to inform customers of the life cycle history of its products. Recently the company joined other major US companies in publicly expressing its willingness to accept carbon emission caps.

A range of social initiatives is also in train (Walmart n.d.). It is noteworthy, however, that there still appear be few substantial initiatives designed to meet criticisms of its relations with communities and with its own employees.

Learning objective 1 in review

1.1 Distinguish clearly between the two different ways in which the term 'sustainable' is applied to business.

1.2 Can a firm be sustainable in one sense and not in the other? Can a firm be sustainable in both senses? Give examples.

The historical development of sustainable principles

The environment was the first focus of sustainability thinking, but it was quickly realised that it could not be separated from economic and social perspectives. A view from the perspective of economic history might find its origin in the work of George Malthus, who, two centuries ago, drew attention to the dependence of a human population on its resource base (Malthus 1798), and in the work of the founding welfare economists, such as Marshall (1890), Pigou (1920) and Pareto (1906), in articulating the theoretical basis of market failure and externalities. On the environmental side, one might point to George Perkins Marsh, a North American engineer who was one of the first to recognise the physical impact of human populations on the environment (Marsh 1864), and to the North American conservation leaders of the first part of the twentieth century, such as Muir (1912) and Leopold (1949).

However, most scholars would point to the appearance of Rachel Carson's *Silent Spring* as the beginning of sustainability thinking in the modern era (Carson 1965). Carson marshalled an impressive array of evidence of the harmful effect of these chemicals on aquatic and terrestrial ecosystems — and of the human health threats, including cancer and genetic damage, which they posed. *Silent Spring* was translated into many languages, and, although highly controversial, was immensely influential. It is credited as having led to the creation of the US Environmental Protection Agency (EPA) in 1970, and to the banning of DDT in 1972.

Not long after the publication of *Silent Spring*, a modest paper appeared in *Science Magazine* by a Californian professor of biology, Garrett Hardin (Hardin 1968). Entitled 'The tragedy of the commons', it became one of the most influential academic papers of modern environmental and sustainability thinking. Hardin examined a fundamental postulate of economic theory, asserting that since the time of Adam Smith, individuals acting in their own interest (to maximise their own utility) had promoted the public interest. Applied to the problem of populations and their shared resource base ('the commons') Hardin showed that this assumption was invalid. This analysis gave rise to a 30-year research program across a range of conceptual dimensions and academic disciplines (National Research Council 2002).

The ecologist Paul Erlich (1968) projected scenarios derived from the mathematics of population growth rates set against the underlying resource base to argue for a dramatic reduction in world population as a means to avoid a radical collapse of both natural and human systems. His thesis was opposed by the management theorist, Julian Simon (1981), who argued that as resources became rarer, resource prices increased and provided economic incentives for discovery. Significant questions remain, however, on the application of this thesis to closed systems, such as ecosystems.

The best-known of sustainability studies is the computer modelling project entitled *The Limits to Growth* (Meadows et al. 1972). This project has now been extended over three decades (Meadows, Meadows & Randers 1992, 2005). The 1972 study centred on a computer model of the world system, 'World3', which was used to simulate different scenarios for the future. It focused on five major trends: accelerating industrialisation, rapid population growth, malnutrition, depletion of non-renewable resources and deterioration of the environment. It modelled limits to agricultural land, agricultural output, the extraction on non-renewable resources and the ability of the environment to assimilate wastes. The modelling was unique for its time in incorporating feedback loops, which are central to describing the nonlinear behaviour of global environmental systems.

The first outputs of *The Limits to Growth* modelling indicated that, if current trends were maintained, within a century society would run out of the non-renewable resources on which industrialisation depends. Overshooting and collapse were indicated, with widespread impacts on whole populations, including massive population declines. Moreover, the modelling indicated that there was no way to ameliorate these predictions by addressing only one, or even some, of the major factors. For example, increasing the resource base causes expanded industrialisation and, ultimately, pollution limits; solving resource and pollution problems leads to excessive population growth and, ultimately, food supply limits. They concluded that growth must come to an end one way or the other. The only decision tree event was whether this would occur by conscious policy and self-restraint or by collision with the natural limits (Perman et al. 2003, pp. 45–7; Tietenberg 2004, pp. 3–7). The 1992 and 2005 updates of the modelling did not deviate substantially from these conclusions.

The conclusions of *The Limits to Growth* were vigorously contested on their first appearance, and that debate has not significantly diminished over time. For example, Simon (1981) argued that the authors of *The Limits to Growth* had seriously underestimated the ability of humankind to respond with creativity and imagination to the challenges presented by environmental limits.

A different critique was mounted by James Lovelock, the founder of what he called the 'Gaia hypothesis' (Lovelock 1989). This hypothesis represents the Earth as a living organism which, like all biological organisms, draws on complex feedback systems to optimise its environment. The feedback loops here are negative, or self-limiting. This is in contrast to *The Limits of Growth*'s loops, which are positive, or reinforcing, of trends. The global environment is thus seen as essentially self-regulating (Tietenberg 2004, pp. 6–7). Human populations, Lovelock believed, ignore these mechanisms at their peril. In recent writing, Lovelock argues that the effects of global warming are examples of just such regulation (Lovelock 2007).

The worldwide concern generated by the founders of sustainability thinking in the modern era found expression in the establishment of the World Commission on Environment and Development (WCED) by the United Nations (UN) in 1983. Its report, *Our Common Future* (WCED 1987), often called the Brundtland Report after its chairman, has become perhaps the best known, and certainly the most referenced, statement of sustainability principles. It ranged very widely over the human condition. The report included:

- a survey of global challenges — predominantly economic and environmental challenges, but also the challenges of poverty, inequality and militarisation
- a review of policy options relating to populations and their human resources, food security, biodiversity and ecosystem integrity, energy, industry and cities
- the institutional changes needed for sustainable development, in the handling of economies, the commons, and peace and security.

The report firmly endorsed the reality of global environmental limits. While supporting *The Limits to Growth*'s concept of linked causal factors, *Our Common Future* goes much further in analysing the scale of these linkages. It observes that powerful linkages exist between the specific environmental stresses themselves; between environmental stresses and patterns of economic development; and between environmental and economic problems on the one hand and social and political factors on the other. Importantly, *Our Common Future* proposes a definition of **sustainable development** that has subsequently been extended to most senses of the term 'sustainability', and is now generally regarded as definitive:

> Sustainable development seeks to meet the needs and aspirations of the present without compromising the ability to meet those of the future. (WCED 1987, p. 40)

As we will see, this is a definition that has been extended to all kinds of sustainability, including those of firms. It should be noted, however, that this statement, which is directed primarily to intergenerational equity, is by no means the only dimension of the concept discussed by the Commission. For example, intragenerational equity is equally emphasised:

> A world in which poverty and inequity are endemic will always be prone to ecological and other crises. Sustainable development requires meeting the basic needs of all and extending to all the opportunity to satisfy their aspirations for a better life. (WCED 1987, pp. 43–4)

Our Common Future has framed the development of sustainability principles and practice for two decades. It put in place the indissoluble connection between the economic, social and environmental perspectives, and it is on this basis that international sustainability discourse has continued. The UN has notably offered a central forum for this discourse through the United National Environment Programme (UNEP). The UN Conference on Environment and Development (Earth Summit), held in Rio de Janeiro in June 1992, attracted thousands of representatives of governments and non-government organisations (NGOs). The Rio Declaration on Environment and Development articulated 27 principles, which are essentially a formalisation of the *Our Common Future* report. There are some new focal precepts, however, including the articulation of the precautionary principle (United Nations Department of Economic and Social Affairs [UNDESA] 1999, Principle 15), a concept which has become increasingly important in sustainability policy over the last decade:

> In order to protect the environment, the precautionary approach shall be widely applied by States according to their capabilities. Where there are threats of serious or irreversible damage, lack of full scientific certainty shall not be used as a reason for postponing cost-effective measures to prevent environmental degradation. (UNDESA 1999, Principle 16)

Another principle which has direct relevance for the idea of sustainable enterprise, as well as sustainable economies, requires the internalising of external costs.

Other major sustainability statements of the Earth Summit were the UN *Framework Convention on Climate Change* and the UN *Convention on Biodiversity*. These joined other UN instruments, including the precursor to the Earth Summit, the United Nations Conference on the Human Environment (the Stockholm Conference) held at Stockholm in 1972 and its *Stockholm Declaration*, and a number of important conventions: the *Ramsar Convention on Wetlands of International Importance* (1971) (central now to meeting the requirements of the Murray-Darling Basin, where there are ten Ramsar wetlands); the UN *Convention on the Law of the Sea* (1982); and the *Montreal Protocol on Substances that Deplete the Ozone Layer* (1987), action under which is now recognised as a major achievement of the international community. More recently, of course, there has been much international attention given to the *Kyoto Protocol* (1997), which made key provisions of the *UN Convention on Climate Change* operational (Fisher 2003, pp. 58–66).

Ever since the 1960s and 1970s, the academic disciplines have been developing to meet the new sustainability challenges. Ecology became a central discipline, and was progressively grouped with earth sciences (such as geology, geochemistry, geophysics, hydrology, soils science and atmospheric physics) together with the new discipline of geographic information systems, in what has come to be called environmental science. It was recognised, too, that the human disciplines were part of the sustainability enterprise (Stretton 1976; Jacobs 1991). Environmental economics, natural resource economics and ecological economics developed through the work of founding figures such as Pearce (Pearce, Markandya & Barbier 1989; Pearce & Turner 1990), Tietenberg (Tietenberg 1984, 2000), Daly (Daly 1991; Daly & Cobb 1994; Daly & Farley 2001) and Common (Common & Perrings 1992; Common 1995; Common & Stagl 2005). Environmental accounting developed in the work of scholars such as Gray and his colleagues (Gray, Owen & Adams 1996; Gray & Bebbington 2001). Environmental law, elaborating on both national and international jurisdictions, became an established discipline (Fisher 2003; Bates 2006). Paralleling a similar evolution in economics (Sen 1987), environmental ethics achieved at least subdisciplinary recognition (Kneese & Schulze 1985; Foster 1997). Academic journals with sustainability orientations proliferated during this period, including: *Land Economics*, *Journal of Environmental Economics and Management*, *Ecological Economics*, *Environmental and Resource Economics*, *Environmental Law and Management*, *Conservation Biology* and many others.

Government agencies have played an important part in developing the principles and practice of sustainability as it is applied to public projects and policy. The US EPA, for example, which was established in 1970, has been both a developer and a coordinator of disciplinary expertise in sustainability matters. In addition, of course, the body has overseen the establishment and implementation of environmental standards and regulations in all the major environmental domains and challenges within the United States. Environmental agencies in most nation states have also shared in this task.

Since the year 2000, and particularly since 2005, much international attention has been on the challenge of global warming and climate change. The Intergovernmental Panel on Climate Change (IPCC) has been the most influential international body in the field, and its series of reports (IPCC 2010) have been widely influential. Following the interlinked global framework described by *Our Common Future*, the IPCC has moved from its initial emphasis on the science of climate change to incorporate economic and social considerations into its analyses. The IPCC's work has been supported and elaborated by national agencies, such as the Hadley Centre in the United Kingdom and the CSIRO in Australia. There is now extensive academic and professional literature centred on climate change and its associated debates.

Finally, it is important to recognise that thinkers and writers about business and sustainability have been active throughout recent history. Some researchers and thinkers have achieved popular status (Hawken 1993; Hawken & Lovins 1999). Increasing numbers of significant theoretical and professional advances in the principles and practice of sustainable business are now being published (Labatt & White 2007; Belz & Peattie 2009; Weybrecht 2009). Much of this work is being featured in professional and industry journals, and in corporate strategic analyses; as well as in academic journals such as those previously cited.

Learning objective 2 in review

2.1 Make a table which tracks the emergence of sustainability principles over the past five decades, with examples for each decade.

2.2 Extract from your table the core set of not more than ten sustainability principles, with each principle stated in a concise sentence.

Sustainable enterprise: core principles for firms

As noted, *sustainable business is the business of firms under sustainability principles.* In this section, five clusters of the core sustainability principles are discussed. Principles are key ideas, concepts and propositions that powerfully define bodies of knowledge and their applications. In sustainable business these principles reach deep into concepts of society and quality of life. Thinking through the implications of these ideas for business is critical to the task of configuring sustainable business practice.

Defining sustainability

As noted, the term 'sustainability' is not well defined in public discourse. Yet for any systematic discussion of business under sustainability principles, the term requires rigorous handling. Here are some current definitions of sustainability.

As noted, the *Our Common Future* report provided the most widely adopted definition of sustainable development and sustainability, framed in terms of *intergenerational* equity:

> Sustainable development seeks to meet the needs and aspirations of the present without compromising the ability to meet those of the future. (WCED 1987, p. 40)

The equal emphasis given in the report to *intragenerational* dimensions of sustainability, in the overriding challenge of global poverty and its associated social justice underpinnings, has also been noted. The combination of three perspectives — the environment, the economic and the social — outlined in this report has come to represent the core conceptual framework of sustainability theory and practice.

There are more technical approaches to sustainability that are defined more generally on the states of systems, comprising the physical, the biological and the human (social and economic) elements. Perman et al. (2003, p. 86) identify six concepts of sustainability that arise from such models:

1. A sustainable state is one in which utility (or consumption) is non-declining through time.
2. A sustainable state is one in which resources are managed so as to maintain production opportunities for the future.
3. A sustainable state is one in which the natural capital stock is non-declining through time.
4. A sustainable state is one in which resources are managed so as to maintain a sustainable yield of resource services.
5. A sustainable state is one that satisfies minimum conditions for ecosystem resilience through time.
6. Sustainable development is a means of consensus-building and institutional development.

Each definition can be viewed from economic, environmental and social perspectives, although these are emphasised more in some concepts than others. For example, concepts 1 and 2 are primarily economic in orientation; concept 5 is primarily environmental; concept 6 is primarily social; and concepts 3 and 4 are a combination of economic and environmental.

An important element of sustainable thought centres on the different notions of *capital*. Under the traditional treatment of financial accounting for business enterprise, capital is identified with the debt and equity funding of firms which are invested in the land, plant, equipment, buildings, patents, licences and other assets that underpin production. The concept can be usefully extended to other kinds of factors that can support the growth of human wellbeing:

- Human capital is the stock of learned skills and productive potential of people.
- Intellectual capital is the stock of knowledge and technology embedded in societies and institutions, including firms.
- Natural capital is the totality of the biophysical systems from which environmental services flow.
- Social capital is the value that resides in social networks and norms of reciprocity between both similar and diverse people.

These differentiated uses of the term 'capital' are not formal definitions. Rather, they are rhetorical devices that are designed to emphasise the fundamental role these dimensions of environmental and social life have in supporting wellbeing. Measuring different types of 'capital' can also help to draw attention to the problems that can arise if these values are diminished. These distinctions come together in an important pair of sustainability concepts:

- **Weak sustainability** holds that there exists a high degree of substitutability between human and intellectual capital and natural capital. Proponents of this view argue for a concept of sustainability in which the sum of human and natural capital is non-declining.

- **Strong sustainability**, on the other hand, while accepting that elements of natural resource inputs have historically been offset by the application of physical, human and intellectual capital, argues that there are important elements of natural capital, such as environmental and amenity services, that cannot be substituted for by human capital.

Economists and management theorists have tended to support the weak version of sustainability; natural scientists and ethicists, the strong version.

Growth and consumption

Underlying all economic activity, including the actions of firms, is the demand for goods and services of the societies and populations they serve. Sustainable business principles, therefore, have their roots in the sustainability analysis of growth and consumption. This analysis reaches into fundamental ideas about society and individual wellbeing.

The view of neoclassical economics

An essential component of the sustainability problem is economic growth. On one side, economic growth is seen as the procurer of prosperity, and the key to any solution of global poverty. On the other side, limits in the global systems that provide environmental services seem to rule out the possibility of unlimited economic growth. This directs attention to the assumption that economic growth is a given in the development of social and economic policy.

Under the assumptions of the orthodox economics— **neoclassical economics** — economic growth makes available to consumption more products and services, both as a proportion of the total and as an absolute quantity. That is why economic growth is seen as a 'good' in its own right. Economic growth is necessary to keep pace with population growth. It increases the material resources available even to wealthy populations, and provides a mechanism for poverty removal in poor populations.

A number of views have been critical of the standard model, which links growth, consumption and welfare. These approaches argue for different ways of understanding national welfare, including sustainability, in the broadest sense, and for different approaches to it.

Sustainability critiques of national economic measures

The value of national economic activity and the outcomes of growth are traditionally related to real **gross domestic product (GDP)**, the output produced by factors of production located in the domestic economy, or **gross national product (GNP)**, total income earned by domestic citizens regardless of the country in which their factor services were supplied. (GNP thus equals GDP plus net property income from abroad.)

These measures have been widely subjected to criticism. For example, the measures do not account for services that are not traded in markets, such as household services or leisure activities. They include the production of some products that do not contribute to, and may detract from, quality of life (e.g. by generating polluting by-products). These effects may fall more on one segment of the population than on another.

In particular, the need for three kinds of adjustment to GNP has been argued (Jacobs 1991, pp. 222–36). The first adjustment is the subtraction from GNP of 'defensive expenditures', such as equipment to control pollution and expenditure to prevent pollution-related illnesses. The second is residual damage to the environment that has not been made good by defensive expenditures. The third is an allowance for the depletion of natural capital, which is effectively a form of capital consumption.

Despite difficulties with arbitrary baselines and monetary valuation of the environment, some attempts to systematise this approach have been made. One of these is the Index of Sustainable Economic Welfare (ISEW). The ISEW is based on 21 inputs, including, on the positive side, an imputed value for extra-market labour services, and national infrastructure, such as streets and highways and public health and education services; and, on the other side of the ledger, urbanisation costs, pollution costs, the cost of wetland and farmland loss, the cost of non-renewable energy depletion, and the cost of environmental damage. On this measure, over recent decades, industrialised nations have shown increasing national incomes, but there have been declines in sustainable welfare from the 1970s onwards (Perman et al. 2003, pp. 648–9; Hamilton 2003, ch. 2).

Growth, consumption and wellbeing

In neoclassical economics, growth and consumption are inextricably linked: increased growth is said to provide more goods and services to consumers. The assumption is that the availability of more goods and services increases consumer satisfaction, and thus contributes more broadly to quality of life.

This assumption has been challenged by a number of researchers (Mishan 1967; McCormack 1996). First, their evidence suggests that the link between consumption and wellbeing is tenuous. Second, it is argued that consumption is actually required for the existence of a growth economy, and is therefore artificially created to meet that need. Third, it is claimed that there are important negative effects of overconsumption that bear on national and global sustainability and on wellbeing.

Hamilton (2003) is representative of these critiques. He begins with the foundational concept of neoclassical economics, utility:

> Open any university (economics) text and the subject is immediately defined as the study of how to use scarce resources to best satisfy unlimited wants. These 'wants' are assumed to be those that consumption satisfies, and the first half of the text is occupied with analysis of the behaviour of consumers in their quest to maximise their 'utility'. By subtle fusion, human beings have become 'consumers' and human desire has been defined in terms of goods; it follows that the only way to make people happier is to provide more goods. (p. 8)

On the critical question of whether more economic growth increases wellbeing, Hamilton suggests, (p. 33) that the evidence is equivocal at best:

> . . . above a certain level of national income people in richer countries are no happier than people in poorer countries; in any given country rich people are no happier than those with moderate incomes; and as people become richer they do not become happier.

Thresholds are important here: as Hamilton accepts, more income clearly does matter to the very poor and to those without food, shelter and healthcare.

These findings are supported by research at the personal level (Eckersley 2004). Subjective wellbeing (the technical term for 'happiness') is associated with social factors: with personal control, self-esteem and optimism; with the ability to set goals and make progress towards them; and with a sense of coherence — a view of the world as manageable and meaningful. Not only are income and consumption conspicuously absent from this list, but the materialistic values they embody are associated with a range of negative effects on wellbeing:

> ... materialism breeds not happiness but dissatisfaction, depression, anxiety, anger, isolation and alienation. Materialistic values go hand in hand with poor psychological health. Human needs for security and safety, competence and self-esteem, connectedness to others, and autonomy and authenticity are relatively unsatisfied when materialistic values predominate ... These values also work against the wellbeing of other people, society and the planet. In short, the more materialistic we are, the poorer our quality of life. (Eckersley 2004, pp. 85–6)

The exercise of consumer choice, which is aggregated as consumption, is a fundamental element of the neoclassical model. Hamilton argues that consumer choice embodies an assumption that is, in fact, never realised: *that consumers come to the market with pre-existing wants and utility preferences.* On this view, the marketing function of business is responsible for the construction of consumer wants. Instead of identifying a market for a product or service, the task becomes one of creating a market. Hamilton suggests that overconsumption is the inevitable outcome of these factors.

Hamilton points out that the environmental impact of increasing consumption and accelerated waste generation is considerable (ch. 7). He cites estimates of the World Resources Institute (WRI) that in the United States, Japan and some European countries, total wastes and pollutants increased by 28 per cent between 1975 and 1996. It has been estimated that over the last four decades, human demand for resources has moved from 70 per cent of the Earth's ability to absorb and regenerate to 120 per cent of its ability to absorb and regenerate. Human populations are now drawing down the natural capital that sustains them.

Theories of sufficiency

Such analyses of growth and consumption have led to the exploration of theories of a steady state, rather than of growth. Importantly, the notion of an economy in neoclassical economics is framed in terms of growth: the idea of a steady state is not considered. Is it possible, then, to think of economic activity — and therefore, by extension, a model of business — which is inherently built on a steady state model? One approach to this question has been through the idea of *sufficiency* and its institutional correlates. For example, Princen (2005) proposes a *principle of sufficiency*, which can become a principle of management and ultimately a social organising principle. It is stated as follows:

> Sufficiency as a principle aimed at ecological overshoot compels decision makers to ask when too much resource use or too little regeneration jeopardizes important values such as ecological integrity and social cohesion; when material gains now preclude material gains in the future; when consumer gratification or investor reward threatens economic security; when benefits internalized depend on costs externalized. (p. 7)

A principle of this kind is necessary, Princen argues, because the critical environmental threats faced by the modern world are unprecedented in triggering dangerous irreversible realities and facing non-substitutable limits that threaten life-support systems. On this view, the driving force is overconsumption, which Princen defines as 'resource use beyond regenerative capacity' (p. 10).

Underpinning this pattern of consumption is an economic, or a legal, rationality. Against this, Princen proposes an *ecological rationality*. The worldview of ecological rationality is one in which the world is, in a sense, ecologically 'full'— it is 'so dominated by one species

(*Homo sapiens*) that life support for that species and others cannot be assumed' (p. 43). Under this principle, one cannot hold to the neoclassical view that the aggregating of individual choices, with respect to private goods, will achieve the common goods:

> ... the 'good' of environmental public goods is natural capital, the ecosystem services that all economic transactions, all economies, rest on ... an ecologically rational society resists trade in its foundations, in the material building blocks and structural configurations that undergird that society's economy. (p. 26)

Rather than individual choice, Princen argues for *collective choice:* 'a group or societal effort that establishes norms, principles, rules, and procedures consonant with ecological constraints' (p. 27). Examples could be the Montreal protocol banning ozone-depleting substances and the work of the IPCC on climate change. This is a sustainability perspective, which Princen sees as having four components:

1. the avoidance of mining renewables
2. a long-term decision-making orientation
3. decision-making at the intersection of the biophysical and social systems
4. the adoption of sufficiency principles as principles of social organisation.

Social justice

The Brundtland Report made clear that the definition of sustainability could not be considered independently of the global patterns of poverty and associated issues of social justice. From a sustainable business perspective, firms must link their purposes and actions to the international commitment for a more humane and equitable global society. This is an extension of the overriding commitment of sustainable business to ethical action.

Sustainability and social justice

The sequence of development of sustainability thought has evolved from environmental, to economic and social, to ethical emphases. The 1990s, in particular, saw the emergence of the social dimension of sustainability. The impact of business operations on local communities, such as those associated with the timber or mining industries, was a focus for business for some time. That concern then extended to labour rights — as in the operations of international sweatshops — and to broader human rights relating to cultural integrity and to viability.

Central to these concerns has been the principle of social justice:

> A more just and equitable world, whether between rich consumers in the West and poor workers in developing countries, between the urban rich and the rural poor, or between men and woman, remains the central concern in the social perspective on sustainability. (Crane & Matten 2007, p. 27)

Social justice, particularly in regard to poverty on the world scale, was the central focus of the seminal report, *Our Common Future*, in 1987. Sustainability principles and practice have built on this foundation, notably through the United Nation's Millennium Development Goals for 2015, which are to:

- eradicate extreme poverty and hunger
- achieve universal primary education
- promote gender equality and empower women
- reduce child mortality

- improve maternal health
- combat HIV/AIDS, malaria, and other diseases
- ensure environmental sustainability
- develop a global partnership for development.

Although high-order goals of this kind might be thought to apply primarily to governments, it is worth noting that some major companies, such as Nestlé, report annually on their contribution to the Millennium Development Goals.

Comparative patterns of environmental and social quality

Developing countries face particularly serious environmental challenges. Environmental degradation in these countries tends to be both substantial and conspicuous. Among other things, developing countries must manage (Field 2008):

- pollution and waste (e.g. emissions such as sulphur dioxide and carbon dioxide; wastewater; municipal solid waste and nuclear waste)
- exploitation of non-renewable resources (e.g. exploitation of oil and minerals)
- the management of commercial forest resources and deforestation
- preserving wildlife stocks and biodiversity at local, regional and international scales
- maintaining the agricultural soil productivity
- development and utilisation of water resources
- maintaining viable levels of marine resources.

Developed countries, too, face the same kinds of challenges. However, they are approaching these issues from a position of relative wealth. In developing countries, the options are much more limited, as the trade-offs in terms of human wellbeing are very difficult.

The disparity on sustainability measures between countries is, simply, stark. The WRI is a Washington-based environmental organisation, funded by the MacArthur Foundation, which collects and monitors data concerning the global environment (WRI 2008). A brief review of some of its reports emphasises the pronounced international differences on broad sustainability measures:

- *Income and poverty.* The developed world of Europe, the United States and Australia reports no people living on less than $2 per day. Rates of people living on less than $2 a day in Asia include: Bangladash, 82.8 per cent; Cambodia, 77.7 per cent; Laos, 73.2 per cent; Nepal, 82.5 per cent. Rates of people living on less than $2 a day in Sub-Saharan Africa vary, with the bulk of countries having over 50 per cent of people living on this amount of money, and many countries having over 80 per cent of people living on this amount of money.
- *Health.* African rates of HIV/AIDS include: Botswana, 37.3 per cent; Lesotho, 28.9 per cent; Namibia, 21.3 per cent; South Africa, 21.5 per cent; and Zimbabwe, 24.6 per cent. These rates are very high compared with the rates in developed countries, which are well under 1 per cent. Per capita spending on health ranges from $4887 in the United States to $2532 in Australia, and to under $100 for the majority of Sub-Saharan African countries. China has a per capita spending on health of $224, and India has an average spending of $108.
- *Food and agriculture.* The US calorie supply per capita is more than the levels of many African countries. The United States, Canada and Argentina achieve net cereal export

percentages of more than 40 per cent; in contrast, Sub-Saharan African cereal imports can be as high as 200 to 400 per cent, and Asian imports can range from 20 to 50 per cent.

- *Water use.* Per capita water use ranges from US levels of 1663 cubic metres to Asian levels of 631 cubic metres. South America has a per capita water use of 474 cubic metres, and Sub-Saharan African has a per capita water use of 173 cubic metres.
- *Population density.* Australia's population density of 3 people per square kilometre stands against Asia's population density average of 135 people per square kilometre (e.g. Bangladesh, 958; Korea, 472). The percentage of people living in slum conditions ranges around the world. Australia has a rate of 2 per cent of people living in slum conditions, the United States has a rate of 6 per cent of people living in slum conditions, Asia has a rate of 40 per cent of people living in slum conditions (e.g. Bangladesh, 85 per cent; India, 56 per cent; Laos, 66 per cent) and Sub-Saharan Africa has a rate of 73 per cent of people living in slum conditions.

The sustainability implications of data like this cannot be evaded. They demonstrate not just gaps on sustainability measures but utterly different qualities of life. One simply cannot compare the sustainability measures of the United States, most of Europe and Australia with the measures of the majority of countries in Asia and Africa. The sustainability challenges to environmental integrity and social life and justice in these latter regions, which include most of the global population, are of a different order: they relate to *subsistence* — to the survival of hundreds of millions, even billions, of people. The trade-offs this situation presents are not only analytically challenging, but are a matter of life and death to entire populations. Modern business, which operates within the global economy, cannot be separated from these realities: it is embedded in them.

The North and the South

Not only is the material standard of living of the developed countries ('the North') greater by many orders of magnitude than the developing and poor countries ('the South'), but the environmental services of the South are being incorporated into those of the North to support the level of consumption — and overconsumption — of Northern populations. For example, it has been estimated that the consumption of the Netherlands rests on the production capabilities of 24 million hectares of land, which is ten times its own area of crops, pastures and forests, with much of this land being in Thailand and Indonesia (its former colonies) (Redclift & Sage 1998, p. 507). Between 1956 and 1970 over half the foreign direct investment of Organisation for Economic Co-operation and Development (OECD) countries (predominantly Northern countries) was invested in raw material production (predominantly in the South):

> The exploitation of farmland, forests, minerals and marine resources was thus seen as a necessary route to economic development — and a degraded, polluted environment [was] an inevitable consequence. (p. 503)

Since 1970, the demands of international capital, aid and debt service to Southern nations is argued to have 'set in motion processes whereby increased demands are made by desperate people on resources to meet their livelihood needs'. This results in unsustainable farming practices: exhausted farmland beyond its limits; increased plantings on marginal land; drawing on common property resources for timber and wood fuel; clearing intact forest for subsistence crops, and so on. (pp. 506–7). The environmental impact of these consumption levels is thus transferred in large part to the South. Jacobs (1991, p. 181) makes this case forcefully:

> Industrialised countries are currently 'exporting unsustainability'. Sometimes this is very starkly obvious, as when toxic wastes are shipped to Third World countries for disposal. But it occurs on a much more widespread basis through the normal mechanisms of international trade. Environments in the South are often degraded in the process of producing primary commodities for export to the North. Fishing grounds are depleted, forests destroyed, soil eroded, wilderness areas despoiled. Even degradation caused by subsistence farming can often be traced back to the displacement of traditional communities onto more fragile, marginal land by landowners and governments oriented towards export. Meanwhile manufactured goods exported by Third World countries are kept cheap (in part) by waiving the environmental standards which would apply in the North. This has the effect of forcing Southern factory workers, neighbouring communities and local ecosystems to pay the costs — in ill-health and ecological damage — which the Northern consumer avoids.

As is now widely being recognised, global climate change driven by greenhouse gas emissions is presenting a new order of international equity challenges. The historical fact is that current levels of greenhouse gases in the atmosphere are largely the product of the industrialisation of the developed countries, and of the consumption which has driven it. Even today, per capita greenhouse gas emissions are much lower in the developing and poor countries. There is even said to be a difference in kind between the emissions of developed countries ('lifestyle emissions') and those of developing countries ('livelihood emissions') (Redclift & Sage 1998, p. 512). Developing countries are thus carrying a share of global climate change impacts arising from the growth of developed economies, but without sharing in any of the material benefits of that growth. A strong case therefore seems to exist for a transfer of capital from North to South, not as aid, but as compensation for environmental damage:

> If the reason that environments in the South are degraded is because of past and present demands placed on them by the North, the 'degrader pays' principle suggests that those who benefited should pay the costs. 'Aid' is then simply a way of internationalising transnational externalities. (Jacobs 1991, p. 182)

The case of modern Asia's economic growth, it may be argued, exhibits both elements: *the right to a historical remedy*, as a recently developed economy; and *the right to a redistributive remedy*, as the manufacturing centre of goods for consumers in developed economies, with all the environmental impacts associated with a rapidly accelerating growth of manufacturing operations.

Case study 2

The North and the South: BHP Billiton and Papua New Guinea

BHP Billiton is the world's largest mining company, with a market capitalisation of more than US$250 billion (June 2010) and earnings before interest and taxes (EBIT) of US$18.2 billion (June 2009). It operates in seven segments (petroleum, aluminium, base metals, carbon steel, diamonds, coal and stainless steel), primarily in Australia, South America, Africa and Canada.

BHP Billiton presents itself as strongly committed to sustainable business practice. In its Sustainability Reports, the company presents the following areas of its business as having measurable sustainability targets:

1. zero harm (fatalities, environmental incidents, human rights, legal compliance)
2. management systems (self-assessment standards, ISO 14001, risk registers)
3. health (hazard monitoring, exposures, occupational disease)
4. safety (classified injury frequency rate)
5. environment (energy and greenhouse, water, waste, land management, product stewardship and Life Cycle Assessment)
6. community (public HSEC reports, community relations, contribution to community programs).

Such evidence of corporate social responsibility is to be commended. It may be noted, however, that the company's Sustainability Reports stand apart from its Annual Reports, indicating that sustainability does not seem to have yet become a core strategic issue. Moreover, it should be recognised that up until a few years ago, BHP Billiton was the principal in one of the worst corporate sustainability breaches in corporate history.

As is well known, since the mid 1980s, the BHP Billiton copper and gold mine in Papua New Guinea (PNG) has released about 30 million tonnes of mine tailings and 40 million tonnes of waste rock every year into the Ok Tedi tributary of the Fly River. Although tailings dams were built in 1983, one year prior to mining, they were destroyed in 1984 by massive landslides, and were never rebuilt. The company sought and obtained an agreement from the PNG government to dispose of tailings and overburden by direct discharge into the river system. The resulting pollution affected the lives of about 50 000 people and seriously damaged ecological systems over 1300 square kilometres. This led, in 1990, to landowners' protests, and to a court action by the traditional landowners against the company in 1994.

The 1996 settlement included a commitment to spend $350 million on the construction of tailings dams, a $90 million trust fund for the people of the Fly River, and $35 million for the communities. BHP Billiton's 52 per cent equity was transferred to the PNG Sustainable Development Program Company, in return for indemnity from future pollution liability.

In reviewing the history of the Ok Tedi Mine, it has been noted:

> The Ok Tedi case was very costly to BHP, both directly in terms of loss of profit and indirectly in terms of loss of corporate reputation. The company failed to recognize changes in their external world; in particular, the increased attention given to matters related to the natural environment in the late 1980s and early 1990s . . . Their organizational routines were apparently concentrated on the technical challenges of ore extraction rather than equally significant matters such as community relations, difficulties with the natural world and the environmental groups who seek to protect it. (Hanson & Stuart 2001, pp.140–1)

Ethical frameworks

Sustainable business is unambiguously ethical business. Ethical frameworks govern all aspects of the firm's operation, across economic, environmental, social and governance arenas. Ethical decision making and action is seen in sustainable business as non-negotiable — transcending even the business case; although, in practice, ethical action can often be shown in the longer term to enhance the economic value of the business.

Sustainable business and ethics

There is a clear business case for ethical business. Acting ethically may enhance corporate or brand reputation, which may, in turn, be reflected in more customers and reduced customer churn. Examples are BP's recent global marketing of its environmental credentials (seriously damaged by the recent Gulf of Mexico oil spill), or Ben and Jerry's promotion of its participatory organisational culture. Reducing energy and water usage is increasingly seen not only as economically responsible, but also as socially responsible. Changing business focus to reduce the risks to the business from climate change is both strategically prudent and socially responsible practice.

At the same time, the ethics of sustainable business also require that firms avoid damage to people or entities, or to environments that others depend on, whatever the business or legal case. Similar moral imperatives apply to the treatment of people inside the organisation. Many would argue that this moral responsibility extends to consumers, suppliers and other constituencies. Moral, or ethical, responsibilities of this kind have been defined as those which 'oblige corporations to do what is right, just and fair even when not compelled to do so by the legal framework' (Crane & Matten 2007, p. 50).

Stakeholder theory

The idea of a firm's corporate responsibility extending to the broader constituencies has been analysed in the stakeholder theory of the firm (Freeman 1984). **Stakeholder theory** asserts the legitimacy of claims on the firm by a number of other constituencies, whose interests may vary widely. In formal terms, stakeholder theory is underpinned by two ethical principles:
1. The firm has the obligation not to violate the rights of others.
2. Firms are responsible for the effects of their actions on others.

These principles generate the following definition of the stakeholder of a firm:

> A stakeholder is an individual or a group which either is harmed by, or benefits from, the corporation; or whose rights can be violated, or have to be respected, by the corporation. (Crane & Matten 2007, pp. 57–8)

In the traditional model there are four groups of stakeholders: suppliers, employees, shareholders and consumers. Here, the shareholders are usually held to be dominant. The stakeholder model extends these constituencies to the wider community of government and community organisations, and even to competitors. The management imperatives that derive from the broader stakeholder models clearly require a balancing of stakeholder interests, rather than an exclusive focus on profit maximisation for the financial benefit of shareholders. Recognising the ethical claims of stakeholders may impose additional economic costs on the firm. Sustainable stakeholder theory asserts, however, that these costs must be accepted as appropriate by owners, even if that reduces return on investment.

Ethical approaches

Ethical practice derives from ethical principles. The frameworks of modern ethics underpin the ways in which firms work through the ethical challenges that are presented to them. This is not a simple matter, but its complexity does not excuse a firm from the task of implementing them in business practice. Fortunately, ethical principles are, in the end, often a matter of common morality, which then simply has to be implemented.

The nature of ethics

Sustainable business, as ethical business, requires an account of ethics itself in order to be able to develop appropriate guidelines and processes. This is necessarily complex, since ethics is a discipline in its own right. Some guiding principles about ethical theory and practice are now offered.

Ethics is about right and wrong. **Ethical practice** is directed by ethical theory. *Descriptive* ethics describes the ethical systems of some society, culture or group of people; that is, how they act without attempting to evaluate the adequacy of their accounts of right and wrong. *Normative* ethics seeks 'to state and *defend* the substantive moral claims' that show how people ought to act. Normative ethics shades into applied ethics, where these basic principles are applied to entire fields, as in medical ethics and business ethics, and to particular issues, such as affirmative action, labour rights or natural resource management (Kagan 1998, pp. 3–11).

Here are some brief statements about the core principles of the major ethical theories.

Utilitarian ethics

Utilitarian theory holds that the moral worth of actions is to be found not in the nature of the actions themselves, but in their consequences. It is characterised by three general principles (Beauchamp & Bowie 2004, pp. 17–19):

1. An action is judged by its contribution to all persons affected. A society should seek always to produce the maximum amount of good, and the least amount of harm, for all those persons. For example, in economic theory, this principle emerges as the criterion of economic efficiency (optimal productivity).
2. Actions under this principle are instrumental: their value is in the pleasure or happiness they produce. For example, this emerges in microeconomic theory as the concept of utility, which is defined as the satisfaction of individual preferences through the purchase of goods or services.
3. It is possible to measure and compare the satisfactions produced by goods and services. For example, this leads to the methodology of cost–benefit analysis — a central approach to balancing stakeholder interests in sustainability issues.

Utilitarian theories are open to some obvious criticisms. Notions of pleasure, happiness and satisfaction are highly subjective and difficult to define. As a result, their measurement and comparison are also subjective and open to individual biases. Most importantly, the distribution of wellbeing within the society or group is explicitly ignored: it is only the aggregate that is considered; the society as a whole. Thus, the special interests of minorities, such as the poor, ethnic groups, children or the elderly, are not explicitly accounted for and may be impaired. The principle ignored here is that of social justice.

Kantian ethics

Traditional Kantian ethics (Bowie 2002) derives moral worth from a consideration of the action itself, not from its consequences. Its founder, Immanuel Kant, distinguishes instrumental actions, undertaken in order to obtain some end, from actions that are morally 'required *per se*, with no ifs, ands or buts' (p. 62). These actions are duties categorically required, as formulated in the three principles of the famous Kantian *categorical imperative* (here paraphrased):

> Act only on principles that could, without contradiction, be taken as universal rules.
>
> The principle has to hold for anyone, anywhere, at any time.
>
> Always treat humanity in a person as an end, and never as a means.

This has been termed the Kantian 'respect for persons' principle. It has direct implications for organisational structure and behaviour. For example, it requires managers to treat employees as 'whole people', rather than as resources applied to business results. In a similar way, it requires a firm to take into account the human realities of its supply base (the sweatshop is the obvious example, but also some purchasing practices of large supermarkets demonstrate this concept). A community or organisation should be so structured that each of its members can act as both 'subject and sovereign'. This principle views a business organisation primarily as a moral community, in which each member stands to the other in an ethical, rather than a contractual, relationship.

Kantian ethics is not opposed to business imperatives. There is ample evidence to suggest that meaningful work, a democratic workplace, truth in advertising and a collaborative relationship with suppliers may well enhance profitability. But the essence of the Kantian position is that the moral imperative comes first:

> Perhaps we should view profits as a consequence, or by-product, of ethical business practices, rather than as the sole goal of business, an end to which all means are subjugated. (Bowie 2002, pp. 70–1)

Kantian theory has been criticised on a number of grounds. It places comparatively little emphasis on outcomes; it requires an optimistic view of persons acting rationally and morally, which, it could be argued, is more the exception than the rule; it does not allow for moral sentiments, such as sympathy and care; and it does not allow for particular or special obligations, such as those that family businesses might argue exist for members of their family.

Rights theory

Despite these criticisms, however, the Kantian perspective has been influential in contemporary perspectives which bear directly on sustainable business. The first is **rights theory**, which has been applied particularly to the protection of individuals from abuse and neglect. Rights are held to be 'natural rights' that constitute human dignity: they are inalienable or entitlement claims which all individuals have, regardless of their membership in any state or social organisation. Key statements of rights have been the US Constitution (1787), the *American Declaration of the Rights and Duties of Man* (1948), the United Nations' *Universal Declaration of Human Rights* (United Nations 1948) and the *Charter of Fundamental Rights of the European Union* (European Convention 2000).

The rights perspective has been particularly applied to the working conditions of workers around the world. It is embedded in industry codes of conduct, inspections, monitoring systems, open-book organisations, occupational health and safety regulations, collective bargaining, training and development, child labour prohibition, and so on. Within modern firms, rights approaches have been applied to issues such as work–life balance, privacy, discrimination by gender or age, whistleblowing and hiring practices.

A second Kantian perspective that has exercised great influence in modern ethics is the theory of justice articulated by North American philosopher John Rawls (Rawls 1971). Rawls develops two principles, or tests, that determine whether an action or social arrangement is termed just. The first requires that if any inequalities are to be allowed, basic freedoms must be realised to the same degree for everyone affected by the decision. The second requires social and economic inequalities to be arranged so that they are to the greatest benefit of the least advantaged, and provide equality of opportunity for everyone to advance their economic and social standing. This has particular application to the key sustainability issue of intergenerational equity (Rawls 1972, pp. 284–92).

Contemporary ethical frameworks

Traditional ethical frameworks, such as those outlined, have been criticised especially over the past 15 years. They have been variously held to be too abstract, too reductionist, too elitist or too rational. More recently, therefore, ethical perspectives have emerged that argue for greater flexibility and for a focus on the particular human realities in which actors, such as managers, find themselves (Beauchamp & Bowie 2004, pp. 31–58).

- Virtue ethics draws on the classical tradition to emphasise personal character and motivation: it is the disposition of a person 'to be generous, caring, compassionate, sympathetic, and fair' that is held to be the true model and prerequisite for ethical behaviour.
- The ethics of care theory argues that, 'Human warmth, friendliness and trust in responding to others cannot be brought under rules of behaviour'. A business thus takes on the character of a 'moral community'.
- Discourse ethics, developed by Habermas (1990), recognises processes of communication and exchange of ideas in resolving the different positions of different values systems, such as those which commonly arise among a firm's stakeholders on sustainability issues.
- Finally, and perhaps most importantly, common morality theories argue that most people understand well, and are broadly committed to, the moral and ethical norms of their community. The legitimacy of these norms derives not from principle but from their proven success, sometimes over centuries, in promoting social and individual wellbeing. Common morality is viewed as foundational, with the authors arguing: 'there is no philosophical ethical theory that takes priority over the common morality; indeed, all philosophical theories find their grounding in the common morality'.

In the application of the theories that embody common morality to practical business problems it is therefore necessary to systematically work through the issues to arrive at a 'plausible rationale' for the theory and its implications:

> If a theory prohibits a certain kind of act, what exactly is it about acts of that sort that makes it appropriate to prohibit them? . . . If a theory holds that morality has such and such a feature, can we explain why morality should have a feature like that? Does it make sense? (Kagan 1998, p. 14)

This process may well involve inspecting assumptions, testing logic, evaluating practical implications, revising theoretical positions, altering beliefs, and so on, until a view of the matter is arrived at that seems, at least for the moment, to be the best available. There is nothing easy about ethical judgements in business. They cannot be evaded, because doing business involves dealing with people. There are also usually no simple solutions. However difficult, ethical issues have to be thought through in sustainable business, so that coherent and just solutions can be found.

Case study 3

Multinational companies and sweatshops

In the global economy, more goods are manufactured and services provided by companies from developed countries operating in the low-cost environments of developing countries, such as Indonesia, Malaysia, India and China. Critics of international sweatshops have alleged ethical breaches, as follows:

1. Multinational companies pay employees in developing countries 'starvation wages': in Indonesia, as little as $1.03 per day, less than the Indonesian government's estimate of 'minimum physical need'. Labour conditions, in occupational health and safety, working hours and child labour, are routinely substandard.
2. Multinational operations have reduced, rather than increased, national income. A bidding war has developed for the business of multinational firms, depressing wages and conditions in a 'race to the bottom'.
3. There is a widening of the gap between rich and poor in developing countries through the operations of multinational firms. The benefits of new operations flow predominantly to local and foreign elites, at the expense of the poor and the vulnerable.
4. Multinationals consistently profit from the repressive actions of governments. For example, the actions of successive military Nigerian governments in repressing the Ogoni people of the Niger delta in order to protect the access of major oil companies, notably Shell, to its oil are held by many to have created a humanitarian and environmental disaster (Newberry & Gladwin 1997).

Surprisingly, defences to these charges have been mounted on ethical and humanitarian grounds (Maitland 2005, pp. 284–9), as follows:

1. The wages paid by international firms are usually substantially higher than local wages. Thus Nike's workers in their Chinese factories are, on average, paid more than a professor at Beijing University. Working conditions for multinational employees are more secure and less hazardous than other workers' conditions in these countries.
2. The costs associated with demands for a 'living wage' or improved working conditions may force international companies to retrench employees or close operations.
3. The free labour market operates ethically:

> The appropriate test is not whether the wage reaches some predetermined standard but whether it is freely accepted by (reasonably) informed workers. The workers themselves are in the best position to judge whether the wages offered are superior to their next-best alternatives. (p. 289)

There are obvious responses to these points. First, despite cultural relativities, there is undeniably an absolute gap in living standards: daily wage levels in the United States could easily be one thousand times greater than the Indonesian wage. The economic value created by Indonesian workers migrates downstream, away from the host country.

Second, higher wages and better conditions will increase costs. However, businesses routinely reduce costs in ways other than retrenchment and closure. Modern ethical frameworks will argue for the treatment of workers in accord with their intrinsic human dignity as a first priority.

The ethical issues relating to business are complex. However, sustainable business does not, in any business situation, resile from the commitment to conduct its operations ethically and to seek coherent resolutions to ethical business challenges. There is nothing easy about making and meeting this commitment, but it lies at the heart of what it means, in the modern world, to conduct business sustainably.

Learning objective 3 in review

3.1 Write two paragraphs that summarise, respectively, the cases for and against limits on growth and consumption.

3.2 Given the complexity and diversity of ethical frameworks, is the demand for sustainable business to be ethical business practical?

The nature of the sustainable firm

When sustainability issues are considered at the level of the firm, a number of questions present themselves. What are the purposes of the firm? What are its legitimate goals and responsibilities? Who are its stakeholders, and what is owed to them? How should it be held accountable by the society of which it is a part, and for what outcomes? These questions have generated a consistent theme of inquiry in economics and related disciplines over at least the last century.

Historical approaches to the theory of the firm and their sustainability implications

The 1930s and 1940s saw the beginnings of a debate about the role of major companies. Four seminal accounts of the nature of the firm are now briefly discussed. It will be seen that what are now thought of as sustainable business issues and concepts have been present throughout this debate.

Berle and Means

The rise of North American corporations presented a challenge that Berle and Means (1932) attempted to address. Firms had moved away from the entrepreneurial model, with its dominance of individual owners, to corporations owned by multiple shareholders and interests. Berle and Means argued that, under these conditions, how a corporation is operated and for whom are questions of real importance.

Three possible structures are identified. Under the first, corporate executives act in a position of trusteeship for the sole benefit of passive shareholders. Of this arrangement, Stretton (2000, p. 362) comments, 'A critical link between self-interest and economic efficiency may be weakened'.

Under the second structure, corporate executives and 'groups in control' are given, by law, 'powers which are absolute and not limited by any implied obligation with respect to their use'. They will contract with the owners for such powers, under which they can 'operate it in their own interests, and can divert a portion of the asset fund of income stream to their own uses'. This is simply 'a corporate oligarchy coupled with the probability of an era of corporate plundering' (Berle & Means 1932, p. 311).

Neither model, Berle and Means argue, can be supported. A third structure is therefore proposed, based on the principle that: *'neither the claims of ownership nor those of control can stand against the paramount interests of the community'* (p. 312).

This is a major statement of principle, and it underlies the modern idea that corporations have from the community a 'licence to operate'. Berle and Means argue that if the community is prepared to put forward its claims, they cannot be resisted by passive property rights: the community is not only a legitimate stakeholder in business, but must always remain the dominant stakeholder. Those community interests may embrace social matters, but corporations must take account of them and allow them priority over commercial interests where these conflict. This is a central principle on which concepts of sustainable and ethical business have drawn.

Drucker

Peter Drucker's 1946 book, *The Concept of the Corporation*, has been seen as a sustained promotion of the corporate model. In it, Drucker also deals with social costs and the social dimensions of companies. He discusses the standard theory of the firm, constructed from the twin concepts of prices and markets, and centred on profitability. Profit, he proposes, is the source of new capital formation, which cannot continue to draw on 'the appropriation and depletion of nature's bounty' (p. 233). The impacts Drucker identifies include soil erosion, depletion of soil fertility, destruction of timber resources, and overconsumption of 'irreplaceable' (non-renewable) fuels. He notes that this trend has been particularly marked in the United States, where there has been 'a veritable orgy of natural-capital consumption' (p. 234). At the same time, economic growth must continue if unemployment is to be held down, and that demands enterprise profitability: 'In a society which accepts economic advancement and economic goals as socially efficient and socially desirable, the profit motive is socially the most efficient device' (p. 240).

This the market accomplishes by providing one standard of values to encompass all human activities and values: making price. The operation of the market, however, must have its limits: 'no society can allow labor, physical resources of land or equipment and money to be treated as "commodities"' (p. 256). The roots of thinking about sustainable enterprise may be seen in two of these categories, 'labour' and 'physical resources of land': 'The market cannot be allowed to destroy them nor to destroy their stability.' The value of a monetary valuation of these assets, however, provides a way of estimating the 'cost to national wealth and income' and 'how great a discrepancy develops between economic and social rationality' (p. 258) — the conceptual foundation of what are now called social costs. Drucker is therefore arguing for an enterprise model based on 'economic rationality', which is centred on prices and markets, but he accepts that society will have to place limits on the operation of these factors to protect the fundamentals of economic advancement.

Friedman

Milton Friedman built on this argument in a notorious magazine article entitled, 'The social responsibility of business is to increase its profits' (Friedman 1970). This article has been endlessly cited as presenting a fundamentalist neoclassical view of the firm, which stands opposed to the idea of a sustainable enterprise. A close reading of the article makes it clear that despite its trenchant language, it is a sophisticated argument centred on corporate governance and its limitations.

Friedman addresses the view 'that business has a "social conscience" and takes seriously its responsibilities for providing employment, eliminating discrimination, avoiding pollution . . .'. He first emphasises that the only responsibility of the corporate executive is to his employers: the owners. Owners will normally want 'to make as much money as possible while conforming to the basic rules of the society, both those embodied in law and those embodied in ethical custom'. There is a recognition here of the idea of the boundaries to the actions of firms set by social purposes.

He goes on to argue that if executives incur costs for the company related to social purposes, they are not acting in the interests of the owner. Rather, according to Friedman, they are 'spending someone else's money for a general social interest', such as improving the environment. Thus Friedman represents a breach of political principle:

> Here the businessman — self-selected or appointed directly or indirectly by stockholders — is to be simultaneously legislator, executive and jurist. He is to decide whom to tax by how much and for what purpose, and he is to spend the proceeds — all this guided only by general exhortation from on high to restrain inflation, improve the environment, fight poverty and so on and on.

Moreover, Friedman continues that it is unreasonable to expect that executives will have any expertise in matters such as macroeconomic policy or environmental policy. In contrast, he argues, it is the market mechanism that underpins the standard model of the firm:

> no individual can coerce any other, all cooperation is voluntary, all parties to such cooperation benefit or they need not participate. There are no values, no 'social' responsibilities in any sense other than the shared values and responsibilities of the individuals.

Friedman accepts, however, that the market mechanism is not always feasible, acknowledging, '. . . I do not see how one can avoid the use of the political mechanism altogether'.

One can respond that the community at large is a stakeholder in the firm, since it collectively owns resources that the firm is using; for example, the common goods of air and water. Its goals must, therefore, be represented in corporate goals. In addition, one can argue that social priorities can align with enhanced business value, a possibility Friedman ignores.

It is important to note that Friedman is not arguing against social goals: he is arguing that firms cannot (by reasons of both governance and expertise), implement them. Social goals, in his view, belong to social governance: they are political and should be set by the political mechanism. To put it bluntly, Friedman is saying if you do not like what firms are doing, to the environment or to employees, you need to gain political acceptance for your views and have them implemented in legislation. Note, however, that Friedman also accepts the constraint on firms of 'ethical custom', which is not embodied in legislation and regulation, and which opens up a demand for ethical corporate action that is very far from Friedman's central intent.

Coase

Ronald Coase's influential articles (1937, 1960) were based on an attempt to answer the question of why firms should exist at all. Coase introduced the idea of 'transaction costs':

> In order to carry out a market transaction it is necessary to discover who it is that one wishes to deal with, to inform people that one wishes to deal and on what terms, to conduct negotiations leading up to a bargain, to draw up the contract, to undertake the inspection needed to make sure that the terms of the contract are being observed, and so on. (Coase 1960, p. 114)

He is then able to argue that:

> that fact that it costs something to enter into these transactions means that firms will emerge to organize what would otherwise be market transactions whenever their costs were less than the costs of carrying out the transactions through the market. (Coase 1960, p. 7)

Markets arise, under this view, just because there are transactions costs: if there were no transaction costs there would be nothing to organise. Coase then turns to the question of social costs. Again the question of transaction costs is central. He models first a system where there are no transaction costs: that is, a perfectly competitive market. Under these conditions, 'people can always negotiate without cost to acquire, subdivide, and combine rights whenever this would increase the value of production' (p. 14).

Coase then goes on to look at the situation where market transactions exist, a closer approximation to the real world. He concludes that under these conditions, it cannot be assumed that private bargaining will automatically bring about optimal results for the economy as a whole. It then becomes necessary for governments to act:

> the activities which they would like to see stopped or curtailed may well be socially justified. It is all a question of weighing up the gains that would accrue from eliminating these harmful effects against the gains that accrue from allowing them to continue.

However, Coase warns against allowing government intervention going further than is justified by the benefit–cost analysis.

Coase has been criticised on many grounds (Babe 2006, pp. 113–14):

- The model of perfect competition is based on neighbouring parties, and does not allow for extended damage, such as that which occurred with the Chernobyl disaster.
- Even under assumptions of perfect competition, it can be shown that the negotiations can take the form of bribes which, although reducing damage per firm, will increase it at the industry level.
- Such bribes can be an invitation to override human rights.
- The size of damage modelled is relatively trivial, and does not take into account scale effects, such as thresholds or limits, on the wider ecological and environmental system.

Economics and the sustainable firm

Under sustainability principles, traditional economic theory has required reconceptualisation in key foundational areas, including the theory of markets and of prices. The extension of cost theory to recognise social costs as well as private costs is central to sustainable approaches to economics. Despite the well-established critique of economic theory made from the sustainability position, and new techniques that have been developed from it, the discipline of economics has yet to incorporate most of its insights into mainstream economic theory.

Firms, markets and externalities

The traditional economics of the firm is directly linked to market behaviour. **Markets** are described as being:

> *entirely composed* of demanders and suppliers, who are real human beings pursuing the projects that interest them, economizing on the basis of the relative scarcities that they confront and negotiating arrangements to secure what they want from others by offering others what they, in turn, want to obtain. (Heyne, Boettke & Prychitko 2003, p. 89)

This is a model of the ideal market, one in which the market process effects an economically successful — and therefore socially successful — outcome by virtue of the exchange it facilitates. **Market failure** is a term used to describe situations where markets are unable to form, or, having formed, are unable to capture all the relevant costs and benefits. Technically, market failures are 'situations where actual circumstances depart from the ideal' (Perman et al. 2003, p. 124), in which:

> Markets exist for all goods and services produced and consumed.
> All markets are perfectly competitive.
> All transactors have perfect information.
> Private property rights are fully assigned in all resources and commodities.
> No externalities exist.
> All goods and services are private goods.
> All utility and production functions are 'well behaved'.
> All agents are maximisers.

When any or some of these conditions are breached (as, indeed, is usually the case), market failure is said to exist. Under these conditions, one response is to 'call for public intervention, either to override the markets directly or to rearrange things so that they will work more effectively' (Field & Field 2005, p. 69); that is, to enact a public policy response.

This analysis leads to the important idea of **externalities**, or spillovers, which are:

> . . . consequences (benefits or costs) of actions (consumption, production or exchange) that are not borne by the decision maker, and hence do not influence his or her action. (Wills 2006, p. 71)

In the model of the ideal market, the economising behaviour of actors in the market is actor-centred:

> . . . individuals choose their courses of action by weighing the expected marginal benefits of any decision against its expected marginal costs. Benefits and costs for other people will not affect the decision unless the benefits and costs for others *matter to the actor.* (Heyne, Boettke & Prychitko 2003, p. 297)

Externalities, or spillovers, are the costs and benefits that are associated with transactions, but which accrue to others, and which are therefore not taken into account when the market actors make their decisions. Externalities are related to imperfectly established property rights of some classes of goods and services, such as environmental services. Thus, manufacturers may emit wastes that impact on the environmental services that system is capable of providing to others. Consumers, such as car owners, may also emit such wastes in operating their vehicles.

In some presentations of this analysis, the distinction is made between **private costs** and **social costs** (Field 2008). Private costs are those which are incurred by sellers, and which relate to goods and services to which they have rights of ownership. For example, an electro-chemical manufacturer would recognise direct costs of metal, chemical, power and labour in producing its saleable product. The intersection of the supply and demand curves under these conditions settles out at a market clearing price and quantity defined as maximum *economic efficiency*.

However, the recognition of externalities entails other costs which are not captured in these accounts. The electro-chemical manufacturer, for example, utilises a government-supplied power and road infrastructure, for which it pays relatively little (corporate taxes do not cover it). Emissions from the manufacturing process may affect air quality and generate health impacts that are paid for by someone else. Social cost accounting includes these costs in total: it is the sum of private costs and external costs. The interaction of the demand curve with the social cost curve creates a different set of conditions defined as *social efficiency*.

When external costs are present, normal market operations will lead to lower prices and higher quantities being produced than are socially efficient. This will result, for example, in increased pollution, relative to the levels of pollution under social efficiency. The economic policy imperative is to require producers of pollution to *internalise* these costs — through a tax, for example — so that they become one of the costs, like raw materials, labour and overheads, that are considered in estimating the most profitable levels of production. This means that firms are required to compensate society for producing pollution. The results predicted by the market analysis are as follows:

> If that makes the polluting activity too costly to continue, it will cease, as it should if its costs are greater than its benefits. If the benefits still outweigh the costs [because paying the tax is less than the cost of reducing pollution], the polluting activity will continue, though at a lesser rate because it's now more costly. But in that case the tax revenue will be available to compensate — to buy the consent of — those on whom the spillover costs are falling. (Heyne, Boettke & Prychitko 2003, p. 307)

Note, however, that under this analysis polluting as such is still recognised as a legitimate commercial action: the question is only whether the firm, or the society, will pay for it. This still leaves the question of the functional integrity of ecosystems out of consideration. Above a certain level of pollution, ecologists inform us, no amount of compensation can pay for the environmental damage, as ecosystems simply stop functioning altogether and cannot be re-established.

The sustainable firm in contemporary sustainability indices and measurement

The result of identifying and internalising costs leads to a different model of the firm — the sustainable firm. There have been contemporary attempts to specify the characteristics and outcomes of the sustainable firm in some detail. One such approach is the *Dow Jones Sustainability Index* (DJSI) (Dow Jones Indexes, Stoxx Ltd & SAM Group 2010).

The DJSI for a company is constructed from what are called corporate sustainability assessment criteria, under three categories: economic, environmental and social.

1. *Economic* criteria include assessments of codes of conduct, compliance and corruption; corporate governance; customer relationship management; investor relations; risk and crisis management; and industry-specific criteria.
2. *Environmental* criteria include environmental policy and management; environmental performance (defined as eco-efficiency); environmental reporting; and, again, industry-specific criteria.
3. *Social* criteria include corporate citizenship and philanthropy, stakeholder engagement, labour practice, human capital development, social reporting, talent attraction and retention, and the ubiquitous industry-specific criteria.

Weightings are given to these 17 factors to derive the DJSI score.

Certainly, the DJSI includes some elements that would normally be associated with sustainability, such as corporate governance, environmental performance and labour practice. However, a number of the elements, such as customer relationship management, investor relations, risk and crisis management, and talent attraction and retention, could equally be regarded simply as standard criteria of good management. Even where a criterion seems unambiguously associated with sustainability, questions arise. For example, the environmental performance criterion asks only whether a company is meeting its own standards of water, waste and energy usage. The environmental reporting criterion simply requires a company to show the fact of reporting, not its adequacy. It is difficult not to conclude that the DJSI is a relatively loose view of corporate sustainability, which may have more to do with corporate reputations in the face of rising community demands and stakeholder activism than a role in rigorously evaluating corporate sustainability performance.

A more persuasive approach is the *Global Reporting Initiative (GRI)*, based in Amsterdam (GRI 2010). Under the GRI, the organisation is required to set the boundaries of its reporting by including the entities over which it 'exercises control or significant influence'. As with the DJSI, the major disclosure categories are economic, social and environmental. However, GRI criteria are more disciplined and comprehensive:

1. *Economic* performance indicators, in addition to standard performance and value measures, include financial implications of climate change, the degree of local operations, and infrastructure investment that is of public benefit.
2. *Environmental* performance indicators include not only absolute amounts of energy, water and materials usage, but recycling and efficiency initiatives. Biodiversity measures look for impacts of operations on protected areas and species, and habitat protection and restoration; and emissions, effluents and waste indicators require specific estimates ozone-depleting substances and greenhouse gas emissions.
3. *Social* performance indicators include labour practices and work practices, encompassing not only occupational health and safety, but training, diversity and employment. It even extends to labour–management relations. Human rights performance is tracked on agreements, screening of suppliers, freedom of association, child labour, handling of complaints and indigenous rights. What is called 'society performance' requires participation in the community, and in public policy development, and tracks anti-corruption initiatives and the record on anti-competitive behaviour. Product responsibility is regarded as a part of social performance: responsibility for health and safety of customers across the life cycle of products and services is required; and labelling and service information is monitored.

This is clearly a comprehensive view of organisational sustainability. It characterises what, from the perspective of the GRI, a company is expected to be, and how it is expected to behave if it is to contribute to the global goal of sustainable development — a goal which the GRI takes to be of critical importance.

Learning objective 4 in review

4.1 Write down in ten sentences or less the core of Friedman's argument on the nature of the firm. Does it stand up?

4.2 Define 'market failure' and 'externalities'. Can you conceive of an economic system without them?

PART 2: SUSTAINABLE BUSINESS PRACTICE

Accounting in sustainable business

Sustainability perspectives move into practical business through the financial impacts of sustainability factors. Accounting concepts have developed to incorporate sustainability concepts and to provide a financial framework within which sustainable business can be effectively managed. Taken together, they challenge the way a modern firm is understood as an entity, as expressed in the conceptual framework that underpins financial accounting.

Triple Bottom Line concepts

Modern presentations of sustainability themes in accounting draw on early work by Elkington (1999) in proposing a Triple Bottom Line (TBL). Elkington identifies seven 'revolutions' in the transition from unsustainable to sustainable business:
1. unprecedented competitiveness for customers and in financial markets
2. a shift to predominantly ethical values in the conduct of global business
3. the demand of stakeholders for comprehensive business transparency
4. life cycle management across the supply chain, from raw materials to production to use and to disposal
5. the emerging dominance of collaborations and alliances as forms of business organisation
6. pressure on all stakeholders to adopt longer time dimensions
7. better systems of corporate governance.

A TBL is offered as a response to these seismic changes in business. The three components of a TBL are economic, environmental and social. The force of the idea lies in the implication that what has, in the traditional business mode, been regarded as the ultimate measure of business performance — earnings or profit — is not the 'bottom' line at all: it must incorporate the environmental and social impacts of a firm's operations. However, a TBL is more an aspiration than a technical framework.

A more recent attempt to give the TBL concept some definitional force was attempted by Gray and Bebbington (2001). They suggest three technical solutions to this challenge:
1. *The inventory approach*. Identify, record and monitor, and report, in non-financial quantities, the variations in natural capital categories under the control of the organisation (e.g. ozone or greenhouse gas emissions, oil and petroleum products, and energy usage and waste disposal).
2. *The environmental sustainable cost approach*. A sustainable organisation is 'one that leaves the biosphere no worse off at the end of the accounting period than it was at the beginning'. Potentially any gap in achieving this criterion can be quantified, and the required remediation costed as a notional addition to operating expenditure.
3. *The resource flow/input–output approach*. Identify and measure the natural resources flowing into the firm's operations, those flowing out, and the losses of wastes and emissions. Physical flows are identified, quantified and given a monetary value, which can be incorporated into notional accounts.

Gray and Bebbington warn, however, that a real attempt at reporting of this kind faces a task that is 'daunting to the point of near impossibility' (p. 315).

Traditional and sustainable accounting concepts

Despite its drawbacks, the TBL concept provides a useful introduction to the accounting treatment of sustainable business. However, it is possible to approach social and environmental accounting more systematically. The analysis begins with the limitations of traditional accounting practice (Rubenstein 1994; Deegan 2009):

- Financial accounting focuses on the information needs of stakeholders with a financial interest in the entity. This limits access to information by the public.
- The principle of materiality has tended to preclude the reporting of environmental information, given the relative difficulty of identifying and quantifying some categories of environmental costs and benefits.
- Measurability is an associated limitation: the recognition criteria of financial accounting require an item to have a cost or other value that can be measured financially and reliably.
- In financial accounting, expenses are defined to exclude the recognition of any impacts on resources that are not controlled by the entity, unless fines or other cash flows result.
- Traditional accounting does not account for the full cost of production because it assigns no monetary costs to the consumption of natural resources such as air, water and land fertility. Social costs and related benefits are ignored.
- Accounting rules may penalise environmentally responsible behaviour by recording only its costs, without its wider benefits.
- Traditional accounting does not have a mechanism for recording green assets, or their consumption; monitoring the use of green assets; distinguishing between the costs of renewable and non-renewable resources; or providing accounting incentives for protection of the environment.
- Traditional accounting does not deal with the idea of inherent environmental limits to economic activity.
- Traditional accounting does not accrue for the low-frequency, high-magnitude risks that characterise adverse environmental events and are routinely associated with the operations of many firms.

Importantly, Rubenstein notes that:

> The traditional accounting entity is the firm. To properly account for air and water, the entity would have to be the firm in the context of the natural capital upon which it is economically dependent, but may not own in the conventional sense of private property. (1994, p. 20)

In the Australian context, a **reporting entity** has been associated with 'any legal, administrative, or fiduciary arrangement, organisational structure or other party (including a person) having the capacity to deploy scarce resources in order to achieve objectives' (Henderson, Pierson & Harris 2004, p. 149). The current International Accounting Standards Board (IASB) draft guidelines propose that: 'An entity is an economic unit that has the capacity to engage in transactions with other entities' (IASB 2007).

Both approaches imply the existence of assets over which the firm asserts ownership and control. Rubenstein (1994, p. 22) notes the limitation of this position:

> The focus is on those things the entity has paid for, on the entity's private property and rights. In other words, the accounting is from the perspective of the owners of the assets. Assets that the entity does not own are not included ... The dilemma traditional accountants face is how to record the consumption of assets such as air or water if the proprietor does not own them.

The net result of these limitations of traditional accounting is that if an entity were to progressively degrade the quality of its supporting environment, then without fines or other impacts on cash flows the performance of such an entity could well be portrayed as very successful. Rubenstein thus proposes the following definition of **sustainable accounting**:

> Accounting measures the economic, intellectual, and natural capital consumed in producing goods and services for trade and for promoting public welfare, as well as the natural and intellectual capital preserved and the wealth created for future use, according to the conventions mutually agreed upon by the stewards of these resources and the stakeholders, in this and future generations, to whom they are accountable. (Rubenstein 1994, p. 29)

Rubenstein offers modifications to the definitions of assets, liabilities and expenses. All three additions require recognition of *natural capital*, the ecosystem services provided by the natural environment on which the business draws as common goods:

- **Assets** include both *the natural capital upon which a reporting entity is economically dependent* and probable future economic benefits obtained or controlled by a particular entity as a result of past transactions or events.
- **Liabilities** are probable future economic sacrifices. Liabilities arise from present obligations or a particular entity to transfer assets or provide services to other entities in the future, as a result of past transactions or events *and the risk of the consumption of natural capital*.
- **Expenses** are outflows or other using up of assets, *including the consumption of natural capital*, or the incurrence of liabilities (or a combination of both) from delivering or producing goods, rendering services, or carrying out other activities that constitute the entity's ongoing major or central operations *(including the preventive maintenance of the natural capital essential to maintain a going concern)*.

Clearly such an approach breaks the nexus between the definition of the reporting entity and the ownership of all the assets used in the business. Here the wider dependence of the business on the common goods of natural capital, and the firm's responsibility for its maintenance, are made explicit.

Social and environmental accounting frameworks in practice

Deegan (2009) presents two practical attempts to implement sustainable accounting. Ontario Hydro, a North American electricity distributor (now Hydro One), pioneered a 'damage function' approach. The damage function was calculated by techniques using market prices to estimate monetary values from those impacts, such as crop losses, that are traded in the market; and using 'willingness to pay for', or 'willingness to accept compensation for', changes in environmental quality for impacts that are not explicitly traded in the market. These estimates were combined with environmental modelling techniques to consider potential damage to the environment. Physical impacts were then assigned monetary value through economic valuation techniques. However, while impacts external to the entity were recognised and valued, they were not fully internalised into the company's accounts, but presented in parallel.

A more radical approach was implemented by BSO/Origin, a Dutch computer consultancy. For some years the company provided environmental accounts, which placed a monetary value on the external environmental costs of the company's operations. Two methods were actual damage costs, and, where these are not available, prevention costs as an approximation. BSO/Origin then deducted the total of these costs (which it called 'extracted value') from operating income, to give what was then defined as 'sustainable operating income', and ultimately, as 'sustainable net income'.

Rubenstein (1994) provides a detailed model of sustainable accounting in the forestry industry. Figure 1 suggests ways in which business performance in this business can incorporate sustainable factors in order to calculate sustainable earnings.

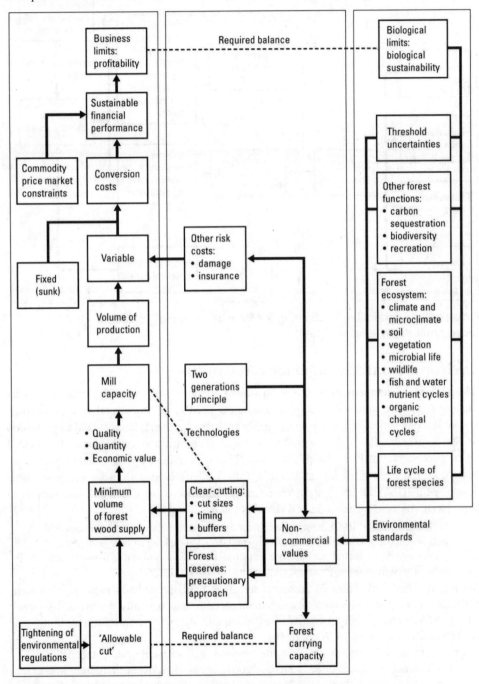

FIGURE 1 Sustainable accounting for forestry: financial performance
Source: Adapted from Rubenstein (1994).

Figure 2 summarises Rubenstein's approach to generating a 'sustainable balance sheet'.

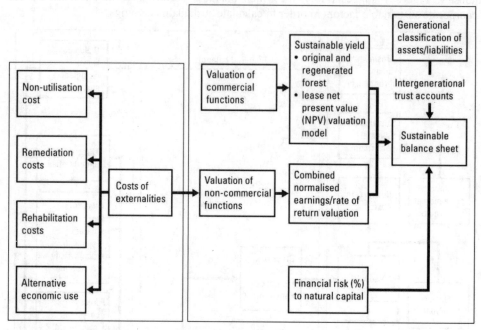

FIGURE 2   Sustainable accounting for forestry: financial position
Source: Adapted from Rubenstein (1994).

Environmental Management Accounting

Environmental Management Accounting (EMA) includes TBL reporting, corporate social responsibility, environmental management systems (EMS), environmental cost accounting, product and production decision making, supply chain management, International Organization for Standardization (ISO) standards, the balanced scorecard and environmentally oriented capital expenditure analysis (Langfield-Smith, Thorne & Hilton 2006). Leading practice in these tasks has been discussed at length by the United Nations Division for Sustainable Development (UNDSD 2001) and elaborated by the Institute of Chartered Accountants in Australia (ICAA 2003). The scope of EMA is as follows:

> the general use of EMA information is for internal organizational calculations and decision-making. EMA procedures for internal decision-making include both physical procedures for material and energy consumption, flows and final disposal, and monetarized procedures for costs, savings and revenues. (UNDSD, p. 1)

The International Federation of Accountants gives these procedures more precise form, explaining that: 'environmental management accounting typically involves life cycle costing, full-cost accounting, benefits assessment, and strategic planning for environmental management' (cited in ICAA 2003, p. 10).

Environmental Management Accounting is concerned with environmental costs:

> . . . material and energy used to produce goods and services (particularly from non-renewable sources), the input costs associated with wastes being generated (including the capital costs, labour costs, materials and energy costs used to produce the waste)

plus any associated disposal costs, storage costs for particular materials, insurance for environmental liabilities, and environmental regulatory costs including compliance costs and licensing fees. (ICAA 2003, p. 11)

A central contribution of EMA to the firm relates to **cost allocation**. In traditional cost accounting the three basic categories of costs are materials, labour and overheads. **Overheads** are indirect material, labour and other costs which are not specifically identified with the cost objective. They can be fixed costs, such as insurance or rates, or variable costs, such as power. There are various methods of allocating overheads, including linking them to material or labour base costs. From the EMA perspective, in practice overhead accounts can hide important information details that bear on environmental performance, and may be specifically related to particular products or services. Costs of energy and water, waste treatment, insurance and regulatory compliance may be of this kind. The management accounting challenge has been expressed as follows:

When environmental costs are allocated to overhead accounts shared by all product lines, products with low environmental costs subsidize those with high costs. This results in incorrect product pricing, which reduces profitability. (USDSD 2001, pp. 1–2)

Waste costs can represent up to 30 per cent of a firm's resources. Waste percentages are often assumed in standard costing, and these may not reflect the reality. In addition, waste costs recognised are likely to be only payments made to waste contractors. Other costs which contribute to the generation of waste, in raw materials, labour and overheads, are likely to be ignored.

The scope of EMA includes:
- determining annual environmental expenditures
- handling product costs and pricing and supply chain management
- managing operations budgeting
- managing capital budgeting
- handling design and implementation of EMS
- establishing standards and indicators, often through the International Organization for Standardization (ISO) series (see later section on 'Sustainable production')
- facilitating clean and eco-efficient production, particularly with respect to energy, waste and water
- handling external disclosure of environmental expenditures, investments and liabilities
- maintaining sustainability reporting
- monitoring reporting to agencies.

Firms are now developing ways to extend these techniques to carbon accounting and carbon risk management.

Learning objective 5 in review

5.1 The conceptual framework of financial accounting is built on the core concepts of assets, liabilities and expenses. How do sustainability principles challenge these concepts?

5.2 What do overhead accounts have to do with Environmental Management Accounting?

Finance in sustainable business

Business finance is being challenged to incorporate sustainability concepts. In both of the core functions of finance — investment and the financing of the business — the incorporation of sustainability factors into standard valuations appears to generate significantly adjusted values. One of the possible outcomes is an increase in market valuation, which is associated with improved sustainability performance.

The business finance framework

The finance function in business has to do with two basic decisions. In the *investment decision*, the amount invested in the assets of the business and the composition of that investment are considered. Assets generate the cash flows that support the business and provide a return to owners. In the *financing decision*, different approaches to generating the funds that finance investments are considered, from internal or external sources. Financial managers attempt to make decisions of both kinds, which add the maximum amount of value to the firm.

The sustainable finance question for business is: Does the explicit recognition and valuation of sustainability factors, such as environmental externalities, have a material impact on valuations and their application to business models and tasks?

Discounted cash flow valuation and sustainability

Contemporary finance theory and practice associates the value of an asset with the cash flows it is expected to generate over time (discounted to reflect the time value of money). The value of the asset is then given by the aggregated present values of the projected cash flows (Damodaran 2006; Peirson et al. 2009). Valuation models of this kind are classified as *discounted cash flow (DCF)* models. As noted, the valuation function is fundamental both to the management of an investment portfolio and to the running of a business (Martin & Petty 2000). When sustainability factors are applied to DCF analysis, the results of the analysis can undergo significant change.

Free cash flow and discounted cash flow valuation

Valuing the entire business, both assets in place and growth assets, generates a *firm or enterprise valuation*. In this case the cash flows considered are cash flows from assets, before debt payments but after the firm has reinvested to create growth assets. These are considered **free cash flows to the firm (FCFF)**.

In accounting terms, FCFF is calculated from the statement of operating income, by adding back in non-cash expenses, such as depreciation and amortisation, to convert it to a cash basis; subtracting cash tax payments; subtracting cash investment in net operating working capital; and subtracting investment in fixed assets.

In FCFF valuation, the discount rate applied reflects the *costs of raising both debt and equity financing*, in proportion to their use — the weighted average cost of capital. The approach therefore utilises three primary inputs: the expected cash flow, the timing of the cash flow and the discount rate that reflects the riskiness of these cash flows. **Discounted cash flow (DCF) valuation** is often called a 'fundamentals' approach: it requires a detailed understanding of the businesses, the drivers of business values, and the likely trajectories of these factors.

Sustainability factors

All of the main drivers of profitability and increasing economic value have sustainability dimensions:

- *Revenues*. This includes income streams from new products and services, generated from new research and development, or from new technologies or new leverage of already existing intellectual capital. Potential pricing premiums may be achievable in the early stages of product life cycles. The re-use, recycling and reclassification of waste have proved to be potent generators of new revenue streams.
- *Markets*. New customer segments and new markets are emerging for products in the sustainability sector. The identification of these markets leads to new value propositions and differentiation; it erects new, and potentially durable, barriers to entry; and it provides the foundation for new branding and reputation capital strategies. New brand and reputation capital can be built around social and environmental citizenship to increase and maintain sales volumes.
- *Costs*. Efficiencies in energy, water and waste are rapidly becoming standard across most industry sectors. More challenging is the implementation of a full-cost accounting strategy, with complete life cycle management. Sustainability risk management now includes not only compliance costs and the costs of managing operational risks, but also wider social impacts and costs. If unmitigated, these costs may be the most expensive risks of all.
- *Business environment*. Emerging global factors are critical drivers of value. The current transformation of the business environment driven by climate change is a clear example. It is difficult to overestimate its potential scale and magnitude.

Financial impacts of incorporating sustainability factors into valuation frameworks

The firm's **value** is derived from projected cash flows, along with expected growth and cost of capital. The impact of sustainability factors is most in evidence with respect to cash flows and cost of capital, as follows:

- *Cash flows*. From the analysis so far, it is clear that one main impact of sustainability factors on DCF modelling will be through new sustainability revenues and costs. These will substantially modify earnings estimates, and hence free cash flows. In a similar way, new capital expenditures resulting from environmental and social mitigation initiatives will modify estimates of net capital expenditure. The associated impact of these factors will modify estimates of working capital, and hence free cash flows. As a result of this analysis, projections of cash flows incorporating sustainability factors are significantly different from projections that do not account for them.
- *Cost of capital*. The cost of equity is influenced by the risk characteristics for the firm, relative to the market. The new sustainability revenue streams flow through the evaluation of business units. Capital expenditures are required to mitigate environmental and social risk flow through to debt levels. Charges necessary to quantify and manage environmental and social risk modify the implied risk premium. Adjustments to these factors generate significant adjustments to the cost of equity. Sustainability factors modify default spreads and, therefore, the cost of debt. When these impacts are aggregated, the valuation utilises a weighted average cost of capital that has been significantly adjusted.

Although risk costs are the most immediately obvious sustainability factors analysts would want to clarify, benefits must also be considered. Increasingly, potential revenues from the sustainability sector are driving valuation differentials, and may be expected to be more significant over time.

Case study 4

Sustainability factors in valuation

One reported Australian case study has looked at the impact on the valuation of including a wider, although still incomplete, range of sustainability costs (Wells 2007). The techniques were applied to an Australian mining prospectus that was seeking investment for a new mining operation. Sustainable finance techniques generated adjustments to the pro-forma financial statements presented in the prospectus. The sustainability costs included mine site costs (such as operational site contamination and spills), impacts on infrastructure of extreme weather events and climate change impacts. The latter were modelled on the Intergovernmental Panel for Climate Change scenarios, and focused on variances in power costs. These are all impacts that accrue as costs, and which affect cash flow projections. Three cases were modelled:

1. the base case, given in the prospectus
2. unmitigated environmental risk
3. mitigated environmental risk (through best-practice environmental hazard management and EMS).

The range of values derived after these adjustments were made suggested that the original projections of potential company and share valuations in the medium-term may have been as much as 100 per cent overvalued. As the impacts of these factors on the cost of capital were not included in this case study, it is reasonable to conclude that the impact could even exceed this level.

Real Option valuation in sustainable business

Uncertainties associated with sustainability factors can thus be handled in DCF valuations through the structure of growth assumptions, and through the tools of risk analysis. Another method of handling uncertainty may be found in the application of Real Option, or Contingent Claim, valuation. Decisions about natural resource investment and development, for example, have been handled through option valuations (since the decision to develop an undeveloped resource is closely related to the trajectory of the price of the resource). This method recognises that firms can learn from developments in technology or markets, for example, over time, and can make appropriate business responses to that learning (Figge 2005; Damodaran 2006, pp. 423–55).

Real Options are those for which there is a right without obligation of a real, rather than a financial, nature. Such options, from the sustainability perspective, may allow a company to carry through a new activity, such as the introduction of a green product, or modification of an activity that has been taken in the past, such as the upgrade of an existing piece of equipment to higher environmental standards.

An example analysed by Figge (2005) is the development of environmentally friendly, fuel-efficient cars. The value of an option is determined by six variables relating to the underlying asset and markets. Under certain conditions, Figge argues, these inputs may be interpreted in terms of sustainability factors:

1. The variance in value of the underlying asset = the spread of estimates for future demand for fuel-efficient cars.
2. The time to expiration on the option = the length modelled by the feasibility study.
3. The current value of the underlying asset = the value of the plan for fuel-efficient cars when exercised today.
4. The strike price of the option = the investments and costs induced by the decision to build.
5. The riskless interest rate corresponding to the life of the option = the interest rate applied to investments withheld during the life of the option.
6. Dividends paid on the underlying asset = the sales of fuel-efficient cars forgone during the life of the option, but realised by competitors.

The environmental management options associated with the operation of these drivers of option value are then:

- *Deferral* options, which allow companies to postpone an investment decision (thus reducing uncertainty), but involve deploying rapid investment when the certainty is sufficient (e.g. the demand trajectory for environmentally friendly cars).
- *Learning* options, where earlier steps provide information that reduces the uncertainty of later steps (e.g. costs and pricing associated with eco-label clothing).
- *Growth* options, where initial investments open up further investment opportunities, if profitable (e.g. new green products introduced in test markets, or new processes, or smaller productions scales, being trialled).
- *Flexibility* options, allowing companies to change processes or products (e.g. changes in environmental regulation, or environmental taxes, or changes in the business or physical environment).
- *Exit* options, allowing a company to exit an investment if an alternatives offer greater profitability (e.g. remediation of contaminated sites to allow ready sale).

The valuation of sustainability-linked assets can then be undertaken by the standard option price valuation methods.

In effect, the DCF modelling values those components of the business, the uncertainties of which do not have option characteristics. The Real Option modelling values those components of the business that have option characteristics. The value of the firm, Figge concludes, can then be constructed as the sum of two components: the DCF value and the Real Option value. The option pricing approach provides a 'fine-grained' analysis of uncertainty. It offers increased rigour in estimating the value of the option to initiate new sustainability activities or modify existing activities.

Learning objective 6 in review

6.1   Give specific examples in a particular industry sector of the categories of the four sustainability factors identified in this section.

6.2   Rank the examples you have chosen for frequency of occurrence, for potential size and for potential impact on a firm in that sector. Do your rankings support the proposition that the greatest financial impacts on firms arise from low-frequency, high-magnitude events, rather than from high-frequency, low-impact events?

Sustainable markets and marketing

The emergence of ethical consumerism and green markets offers new niches for competitive advantage and, as social norms change, may mark the early stages of a wholesale shift in the markets of some industries. These new markets present new opportunities for competitive differentiation, through both positioning and price. Social marketing is a new marketing discipline that has emerged primarily to support programs for changing household or firm behaviour in more sustainable directions.

Customers and markets

Drucker (1968, p. 91) conceives of business as 'a process which converts a resource, distinct knowledge, into a contribution of economic value in the market place', and therefore concludes that, 'The purpose of a business is to create a customer'. Every business, he continues, is actually defined in terms of the customer, or of their aggregation in markets or of end users. This is explicitly a view from outside the business: '. . . the most important questions about a business are those that try to penetrate the real world of the consumer, the world in which the manufacturer and his products barely exist' (p. 101).

On this view, the strategic task begins with the identification of the customer, and an understanding of the ways in which the customer assigns value to products and services. This forces the businessman to

> take action according to the logic of the market, rather than according to the logic of the supplier. He must adapt himself to the customers' behaviour if he cannot turn it to his advantage. Or he has to embark on the more difficult job of changing the customer's habits and vision. (p. 108)

The primacy of the market in developing business strategy is being asserted here, with uncompromising firmness. The business is not driven primarily by its products and services but by the customer's values, satisfactions, and even rationality:

> . . . forcing oneself to respect what looks like irrationality on the customer's part, forcing oneself to find the realities of the customer's situation that make it rational behavior, may well be the most effective approach to seeing one's entire business from the point of view of the market and the customer. (p. 110)

In the traditional industry organisation model of strategy, this perspective appears as *strategic market segmentation*, defined as follows:

> . . . recognising the subdivisions that either naturally exist in the market or can be created within the market and appropriately aligning the company's business processes and resources to most efficiently satisfy those segments that best fit with the firm's advantages. (Davis & Devinney 1997, p. 182)

The potential market is first segmented by demand variables of the kind Drucker advocates, such as customer needs, wants, benefits sought, solutions to problems desired and so on. These segments are described by variables that assist in understanding how to serve these customer needs, such as demographics, psychographics, behaviour, decision making and media patterns. Targeting and selection of segments is followed by positioning the firm's products and services for greatest advantage to the selected customer segments (Davis & Devinney 1997, ch.7). The ability to see these patterns clearly and to align the firm's business processes with them is a key determinant of business success.

Recent empirical work suggests that in certain markets and product groups there has been a significant growth of *ethical consumerism* (MacGillivray 2000; Crowe & Williams

2001; Tallontire 2001). For example, a study of purchases of major household items (Tallontire 2001) found a growth rate of over 30 per cent in ethical purchases in the period 1999–2000, with certain categories, such as fuel and light, and transport, achieving much higher growth rates (74 per cent and 42.5 per cent respectively). Although the base is small (probably only a few per cent at most) these growth rates are impressive, and seem to be sustained.

Tallontire (2001) found three main value drivers of the ethical consumer segment: the environment, animal welfare and human rights (including working conditions and Fairtrade). Crowe and Williams (2001) identified five categories of consumers with respect to ethical consumerism, with three in particular accounting for almost all of the variability:
1. No significant ethical concern (more than 50 per cent)
2. Main focus on value for money (20 per cent)
3. Young consumers not set in purchase behaviour patterns
4. Ethically concerned non-activist group (20 per cent)
5. Ethically concerned activist group.

Of these, the last two groups are relevant to sustainable business. The fourth group, ethically concerned non-activists, are defined by a readiness to buy or avoid products on ethical grounds, if the issues are obvious and information about them is readily available. These consumers do not feel guilty about purchasing non-ethical goods, but they do seek out information on ethical issues. They are likely to claim to prefer ethical goods, but to still defer to other factors, such as relative price, when making purchasing decisions. The fifth group, ethically concerned activists, comprises consumers who are likely to rank social and environmental issues above other factors, such as brand names. They will actively seek out ethical labels, such as those indicating recycled, genetic-modification free (MacDonald & Whellams 2007), or Fairtrade goods. They are also active in seeking out information that regularly guides them in buying or avoiding certain products. These findings indicate that there is potential for at least a proportion of the relatively large fourth group to migrate to the more engaged status of the fifth group (Wheale & Hinton 2007).

Studies such as these reflect changing trends in social attitudes or norms. In the early stages of such trends, profitable niches are often available. Focusing on ethical consumerism, differentiation according to the environment, Fairtrade, animal rights and welfare or employee welfare (or a combination of these), for example, can give products ethical dimensions. Firms targeting these segments and product niches attempt to distance themselves from less ethically oriented firms. Firms that do not position themselves on ethical dimensions can experience serious consequences in the market: recent reports suggest that many hundreds of products are currently subject to consumer boycotts worldwide (Wheale & Hinton 2007).

In addition to particular products, firms themselves can be evaluated by consumers on the basis of sustainable or ethical practices. For the more activist segment, this may extend to the firms that occupy different positions in the supply chain. For example, suppliers of raw materials may interact with local populations in ways that are unacceptable to ethical consumers. Processors may adopt manufacturing processes that are polluting, or employ labour under unacceptable conditions. As ethical consumers become more knowledgeable and more demanding of acceptable practices, firms can be expected to find themselves being held accountable not only for their own products, business processes and practices, but also for their suppliers' products, processes and practices, as in Nokia's monitoring of its Chinese suppliers.

Market research has begun to deliver a fine-grained analysis of ethical consumerism. Wheale and Hinton (2007) analysed a survey completed by 250 readers of the quarterly *Ethical Consumer Magazine*. It was reasoned that readers of this magazine would be representative of ethical consumers in groups four and five (discussed earlier in this section) — those who 'actively seek information to aid in the purchase of ethically associated goods'. The study first examined potential differences in strength of feeling across three main ethical issues: environmental issues (pollution, nuclear power, ozone depletion, acid rain and so on); human rights (workers' rights, oppressive regimes, armaments, selling policy, child labour and so on); and animal rights/welfare (testing, factory farming, animal welfare and so on). The study further examined differences in strength of feeling between and within product groups across the three main ethical issues. Product groups included food goods, toiletries, clothes, white goods, brown goods and cars. The findings of the study suggested that the environment was the highest ranked issue, followed by human rights and then animal rights/welfare. Food, toiletries and white goods were more likely to be ethically evaluated than brown goods, cars or clothes. There was evidence that consumers evaluated the product categories differently; that is, the ethical bundles or profiles applied differed significantly from group to group.

Importantly, it was noted that the potential outcomes of such a strategy can help a firm to meet its responsibility to its shareholders, as well as, in cooperation with similar companies, its responsibility to the wider community:

> For those companies willing to embrace the challenge of identifying what ethical drivers are associated with ethical consumer markets and supplying consumers with products that are commensurate with them, not only should they ultimately gain a competitive advantage over their more complacent rivals ... but together such companies can make an invaluable contribution to the wellbeing of the environment, human rights and animal welfare. (Wheale and Hinton 2007, p. 314)

Marketing under sustainability principles

Marketing academics are increasingly turning their attention to the impact of sustainability principles on marketing theory and practice. Belz and Peattie (2009, p. 18) present one approach to this task. The outcomes of what is called **sustainability marketing** are marketing solutions that are:

1. *ecologically oriented*: satisfying consumer needs within the limits of ecological systems
2. *viable*: delivering competitive economic outcomes
3. *ethical*: promoting social justice and equity
4. *relationship-based*: conceived of in terms of relationships with customers and stakeholders, rather than in terms of simple economic exchanges.

The first three criteria are familiar from the previous discussion. The fourth criteria relates principally to the marketing context, although it has conceptual roots in social economic thought, where human needs are understood much more broadly than in classical economics, and extend to human rights, higher needs (the wholeness of the person), and ultimately human dignity (Lutz 1999). It also derives from the contemporary realisation, particularly in the internet age, that collaborative relationships in all phases of business are becoming increasingly critical to competitive positioning.

Belz and Peattie go on to identify several key elements in marketing under sustainable principles: socio-ecological problems, consumer behaviour, sustainability marketing values and objectives, the sustainability marketing mix and the sustainability marketing transformation. These elements embrace the external environment, the corporate level, the product level and the institutional level (p. 31).

At the customer level, Belz and Peattie note that sustainability principles must be applied across the trajectory of consumption. At the pre-purchase level, sustainable products and services are 'offerings that satisfy customer needs and significantly improve the social and environmental performance along the whole life cycle, in comparison to conventional or competing offers' (p. 154).

This general principle is applied to the delivery of customer satisfaction and environmental and social outcomes across the life cycle, as well as to competitive positioning. Fairtrade products are cited as examples (p. 155). Production is explicitly included in these principles.

At the customer use level, the safety and health of products is emphasised, as in the replacement in India of polluting, open-cooking fires by wood-burning fires designed to reduce pollution. Energy and water use become critical, leading to the demand for ratings displayed prominently in white goods. Increased durability and the absence of planned obsolescence reduce the environmental impact of raw materials extraction and processing. Willingness to share can become a crucial factor, as in home gardening equipment. At the consumer post-use level, the issue of safe disposal, recycling or re-use becomes central. These are discussed further in the next section.

Belz and Peattie also discuss the emergence of sustainability brand positioning. This is now a ubiquitous element of the marketing toolbox. It has moved from whole companies, such as The Body Shop, to individual products and services, under the general branding of 'green'. There is an emerging view that this branding may be becoming increasingly damaged as a brand category by products and services that do not meet the standards that they are claiming to meet, or the standards that the public perceive should be associated with this brand. 'Greenwash' is the generic term applied to these deceptive tactics (Clegg 2009). The annual sustainability reports issued by many companies are a case in point. By holding these reports separate from the annual financial reports, companies thus avoid the difficult task of quantifying the financial implications of sustainability reports and of modifying the annual financial reports accordingly. In this way, these companies escape the scrutiny of auditors being applied to their sustainability performance, while claiming that they are a sustainability or green brand. It should be noted that when corporate green brands collapse, their impact can be devastating. The retreat of The Body Shop from its founding sustainability principles is an example, as is the impact of the Gulf of Mexico oil spill on the green BP brand.

Social marketing

In recent years the potential value of applying professional marketing techniques to producing social and environmental behavioural change has been explored. This international initiative has given rise to the new discipline of **social marketing**, defined as follows:

> Social marketing is the application of commercial marketing technologies to the analysis, planning, execution, and evaluation of programs designed to influence the voluntary or involuntary behaviour of target audiences in order to improve the welfare of individuals and society. (Donovan & Henley 2003)

Social marketing campaigns are undertaken through a disciplined sequence of activities (McKenzie-Mohr & Smith 1999; Kotler, Roberto & Lee 2002; Donovan & Henley 2003) that are outlined in figure 3.

1. Planning	2. Research and analysis
• Determine program focus. • Identify campaign purpose. • Establish specific, realistic and measurable objectives. • Review existing research and practice. • Map out a program prototype. • Establish checkpoints for making go/no-go decisions. • Select broad outcome measures to judge progress and success.	**Consumer analysis** • Conduct and analyse quantitative/qualitative research. • Identify target population segments. • Study consumer motivational and resistance points (benefits and barriers). • Analyse the competition. **Market analysis** • Designate the marketing mix (product, price, place and promotion). • Examine target group/current product fit. • Identify competitors and allies. **Channel analysis** • Examine communication channels against target audience and program goals. • Assess available vehicles. • Seek potential collaborating organisations.
3. Social marketing strategies	**4. Social marketing management**
Marketing mix strategy • Translate the marketing mix into a program strategy. • Test concepts and product prototypes with the target group. • Market test the strategy in a focused area and refine the strategy. **Communication** • Clarify ideas and information and develop pilot messages. • Test concepts and message strategies with the target group and refine the concepts and strategies. • Produce, test and refine communication materials.	**Detailed implementation planning** • Develop implementation plan, including activities, accountability, timelines, milestones, budgets and evaluation. **Implementation** • Secure involvement and commitment of collaborators. • Train key members in execution and delivery. • Activate communication and distribution. **Process evaluation** • Assess quality of target group exposure to program communications. • Evaluate the delivery of the product or service. • Obtain data on product use. • Modify product/distribution/communication. **Outcome evaluation** • Assess validity of evaluation methodology. • Assess program impact through statistical comparisons using the preselected outcome measures. • Estimate cost-effectiveness of the program.

FIGURE 3   Social marketing dimensions

Case study 5

Social marketing

The Global Action Plan for the Earth (GAP) focuses on international participation in household environmental behaviour change (Kassirer & McKenzie-Mohr 1998; Empowerment Institute 2004). Founded in 1989 in New York State as a non-profit organisation, the GAP Community Lifestyles Campaign, aimed at households, has been implemented on a wide international scale. The program was aimed at adults. By 2004 it had been applied in 17 countries, with the participation of over 150 000 people, more than 80 000 of whom were living in the United States (Global Action Plan 1995).

The GAP program targeted innovator communities that had expressed interest and a willingness to provide financial support. Availability of recycling information was a criterion used to identify these 'early adopter' neighbourhoods. It was estimated that these neighbourhoods represented approximately 15 per cent of the total population. Citizen participation was achieved by identifying motivated individuals in the neighbourhoods, and helping them to reach out to other neighbours to build peer support groups, called EcoTeams. These teams met eight times over four months, with the help of a step-by-step workbook and a trained volunteer coach. Choosing from a series of practical actions — each chapter in the workbooks covered seven to 12 activities that participants could undertake — the individuals of a team supported one another to reduce waste, use less water and energy, buy eco-wise products (waste reduction), and reduce air and water pollution. Members of each EcoTeam logged their activities, shared them at subsequent meetings, and finetuned plans going forward. The program was financed by a $35 membership fee.

Word-of-mouth recruiting was central: members of teams encouraged other neighbours to get involved. In the United States, 40 to 50 per cent of neighbours approached to attend an introductory event agreed to do so; 85 per cent of attendees at this event joined EcoTeams. In addition, partnerships were developed with municipalities to launch and manage the start-up program, and to customise the program to fit local conditions and needs. A national body, The President's Council on Sustainable Development, helped with promotion and recruiting; a partnership was also developed with the United National Environment Program in North–South dimensions of household sustainability.

Results of the program were generally encouraging. For example, in a study of the EcoTeam in Issaquah, Canada, 87 per cent of members indicated that participating in the program had helped them go to their next level of sustainable living; 45 per cent reported that they transferred knowledge from the program to their workplace; 26 per cent extended their environment volunteer work to other community activities; and 13 per cent had supported approaches to government in favour of sustainability initiatives (Issaquah EcoTeam1998). Average resource savings per year across the international GAP program were reported as shown in table 1.

TABLE 1 Average resource savings per year across the GAP program

	International	United States
Reduced waste production (%)	35–51	42
Reduced water consumption (%)	25–34	25
Reduced energy consumption (%)	16	16
Reduced fuel (%)	16–20	16
Annual savings per household ($)	227–389	400

Source: Harland (1995); Staats and Harland (1995).

A two-year government study in the Netherlands found that 46 out of a possible 93 environmentally relevant behaviours were implemented by 205 EcoTeam participants over six to nine months following completion of the program. Participation remained high across a range of community contexts, and even resulted in the improvement of the household behaviours targeted.

Learning objective 7 in review

7.1   In your experience, is the green consumer consistent across categories of goods and services? How would you design a market research study to find out?

7.2   Reducing domestic water usage is critical to many countries, including Australia. Design the main elements of a social marketing campaign to achieve this outcome.

Sustainable production

Production systems occupy the most visible position in sustainable business. It is the impact of production processes on the environment, particularly in manufacturing, which is most directly associated by the public at large with the demand for sustainable business. Modern approaches to sustainable production extend across the three pillars of sustainability — economic, environmental and social — and are increasingly regulated. In response to these demands, a range of well-known international codes have been developed, and these are now regarded as standard in the operations of manufacturing and other production systems.

The legislative and regulatory environment

All firms operate within a legal and regulatory environment. Some of these legal structures relate to the ways in which firms as incorporated entities operate within the society: in Australia, the *Corporations Act 2001* (Cwlth) fulfils this role (Cassidy 2003). Other legislation relates specifically to the sustainability dimensions of business: the *National Environment Protection Act 1994* (Cwlth) regulates the handling of pollution in Australia. In certain industries, codes have the force of regulation: the Building Code of Australia includes specifications for a range of sustainability factors in materials and design (Australian Building Codes Board 2008).

The first requirement for sustainable business production is compliance with these complex, overlapping regimes. It has been argued that sustainable business is more than compliance. However, there is no doubt about the need for compliance: regulatory breaches of sustainability requirements can have substantial business impacts, through fines, compensation, legal costs and loss of reputation.

Pollution remains the primary production focus of legislation and regulation. The dominant method of reducing pollution has been through the use of *command and control* instruments. A useful classification of these instruments, and the elements of the production process causing the pollution, is provided in figure 4. Looking at figure 4, it is apparent there are command and control instruments that are applied by regulation to each stage of the production process.

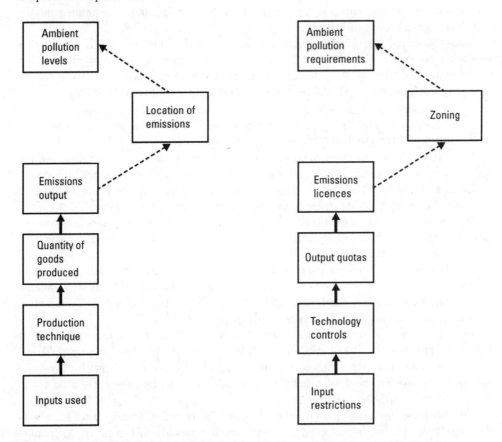

FIGURE 4 A flowchart of production and pollution and the command and
control instruments

Source: Adapted from Perman et al. (2003, p. 210).

In Australia, regulations for environmental protection, within which businesses operate, are embedded in overlapping federal and state legal structures. At the *national* level, policies for pollution control are developed by the Environment Protection and Heritage Council (EPHC), based on a 1994 agreement between the Commonwealth and the States to develop a coordinated approach to the formulation and implementation of environmental policies. The role of the EPHC is restricted to the development of **National Environment**

Protection Measures (NEPMs). These measures can take the form of standards, goals, guidelines or protocols. National Environment Protection Measures can only be made with respect to specific areas, such as ambient air and water quality, re-use and recycling, motor vehicle noise and emissions, and guidelines for assessment of site contamination. 'Ambient' pollution is dispersed pollution that is not limited to, or identified with, specific point sources (e.g. urban air pollution). The EHPC has no responsibility for the regulation of 'point-source' pollution, which is pollution that is identified with specific locations as sources (e.g. wastes escaping into the environment from a factory or a farm). Hence, the EHPC has no direct regulatory control over firms or individuals. This control is exercised at state level. The States, however, are required to develop legislation to implement the NEPM in their respective jurisdictions.

Bates (2006, pp. 389–90) notes that *state* legislation has moved its focus from earlier legislation, developed in the 1960s and 1970s, which focused on the effect of emissions on the receiving environment, to regulating the processes that cause pollution. An important concept in this legislation is **Best Practice Environmental Management (BPEM)**:

> environmental management of an activity which achieves ongoing minimization of environmental harm through cost-effective measures assessed against measures currently used nationally and internationally for that activity. (p. 396)

Best Practice Environmental Measures vary widely from industry to industry, and are often embodied in industry arrangements of various kinds, which are regularly monitored, evaluated and updated. These may include *codes of practice*, as in the Building Code of Australia. *Industry plans and agreements* may also be developed: the state of Victoria has recently introduced 'sustainability covenants', which can be entered into between the Environmental Protection Agency and an industry to increase resource use efficiency, or to reduce ecological impact.

The development of uniform *environmental standards* has been historically important in Australia. Here the BPEM systems may be applied through the **Best Available Technology Economically Achievable (BTEA)**, which is the best technology for pollution control currently in use or commercially available (pp. 450–506).

Licensing is a key control strategy. The licensing legislation may refer to particular industries, processes or industries; for example, agricultural feedlots, mining gold and milling of pulp and paper. Licences are organised by level, so that a low-level environmental risk may be dealt with by local authorities, with higher-level risks dealt with by state agencies (pp. 407–14).

Environmental protection orders or notices may be issued to ensure compliance with the legislation or its instruments, to abate environmental nuisances or to require remediation. *Abatement notices* can be issued to require activities that are causing pollution to be prevented or modified. Offensive noise, air emissions and waste discharges are examples of such activities (pp. 420–3).

The Environmental Management System

From a legal perspective, the **Environmental Management System (EMS)** is

> a corporate system for pollution prevention that informs management and employees at all levels of an organisation how to approach their pollution prevention responsibilities. It establishes chains of communication with the organisation so

that prompt and effective responses can be made if anything does go wrong. (Bates 2006, p. 406)

Standards Australia has adopted the ISO 14000 series as the framework for EMS in Australia. The ISO 14001 standard deals specifically with EMS. The EMS seeks to incorporate into its framework all significant environmental impacts, and thereby to improve upon and minimise such impacts (Whitelaw 2004, p. 3).

The overriding goal of ISO 14001 is require a firm 'to control and reduce its impact on the environment'. In particular, the Standard

> requires an organization to state how it goes about controlling and reducing its impact on the environment; doing in practice what it has stated in its environmental policy; recording what has occurred; and learning from experience. (p. 5)

It is recognised by the Standard that meeting all the legislative and regulatory requirements that relate to a firm's environmental performance is a primary foundation of the EMS. In addition, however, the Standard addresses the needs of firms who seek to go

> beyond those legal requirements in order to ensure that their environmental integrity (of activities, products and services) meets the expectations of the stakeholders. (p. 5)

It is also important to note that the ISO 14001 is fundamentally based on the principle of *continuous improvement*. There are six clauses which govern the ISO 14001 standard:

1. *Clause 4.1: General requirements.* There must be objective evidence that the EMS is in place and is being regularly reviewed and revised through meetings and audits.
2. *Clause 4.2: Environmental policy.* A statement of corporate policy on environmental outcomes applies across all levels of management, is transparently developed and is publicly accessible.
3. *Clause 4.3: Planning.* The planning process identifies and ranks actual and potential environmental impacts of the firm's operations, both direct and indirect (through a supplier or a customer) and develops clear, achievable objectives, measured by specific targets, both short and long term.
4. *Clause 4.4: Implementation and operation.* Firm personnel are assigned specific responsibilities and made directly accountable for particular tasks under a well-defined reporting structure. Training needs are identified, together with measures of competence. Communications structures are established, both internally (with employees) and externally (with stakeholders, including complainants). A minimum level of documentation, focusing on the main elements, is developed. Operational control is established. Emergency plans are developed.
5. *Clause 4.5: Checking and corrective action.* Checking verifies that the planned actions and activities are taking place and are producing the expected improvements. Gaps in either area are met with timely corrective action.
6. *Clause 4.6: Management review.* Senior management meet regularly to determine whether the firm is doing what it said it would do, and achieving its objectives and targets. In the event of gaps, causal factors are determined and corrective actions taken.

An example of an industry code which has been developed on the platform of the ISO 14001 standard is the Code of Environmental Practice of the Australian petroleum exploration industry (Australian Petroleum Production & Exploration Association 1996). By contrast, an example of an industry code which provides general sustainability principles (rather than using the ISO platform) is the framework of the Minerals Council of Australia (2005).

Case study 6

Environmental management system implementation in Italy

Alberti et al. (2000) examined the costs and benefits of EMS implementation in a sample of 14 companies out of 160 which had adopted ISO 14001 in Italy. Their findings were:

- *Costs. Implementation costs* were the resources needed to plan and document the EMS, conduct the preparatory environmental analysis and assessment, procure instrumentation, develop or hire professional skills, implement the system, and implement remediation where appropriate. *Certification costs* were the direct costs of the certification and surveillance visit, together with the internal audit and re-assessment. *Maintenance costs* were the costs incurred by cleaner materials or products and cleaner technologies, EMS surveillance, and the ongoing requirements of the Standard, including training, monitoring and control, and document management.

- *Benefits. Economic benefits* included raw materials conservations, reduced accidental events, re-use of rejects, energy consumption reductions, reduced logistic costs and reduced idle time from risk reduction. Waste reductions, and waste treatment or transport costs, were markedly improved. Improved access to insurance was also noted. In many cases these were not large effects — often 2 to 4 per cent — but the significant volumes affected generated substantial financial improvements. *Non-economic benefits* included better knowledge of the job and its risks, reduced legal liabilities, improved company image and credibility with the general public and with public agencies, and a better product image with customers. Reduction in the risk of serious accidents and human consequences was significant. New market opportunities opened, in establishing a qualification for a supply contract, or in the criteria for evaluation of potential suppliers. Social costs, too, were identified, in the average reductions in air pollutants of 8.7 per cent, and in the projected long-term beneficial impact on occupational diseases.

It was estimated that the aggregate annual costs, both capital and operational, for application of the EMS was between 0.5 and 1.5 per cent of sales, with a payback period of between 18 and 24 months.

Life Cycle Assessment

Life Cycle Assessment (LCA) is a pivotal concept of sustainable enterprise practice. A useful summary of this work has been provided by the US EPA (Scientific Applications International Corporation 2006), from which the outline that follows is mainly drawn. *Life Cycle Assessment* is an approach to assessing the environmental impact of industrial systems. The life cycle encompasses

> the major activities in the course of the product's life span from its manufacture, use, and maintenance, to its final disposal, including the raw material acquisition required to manufacture the product. (p. 1)

The phrase 'cradle-to-grave' is also widely used to describe LCA. Figure 5 summarises the Life Cycle stages.

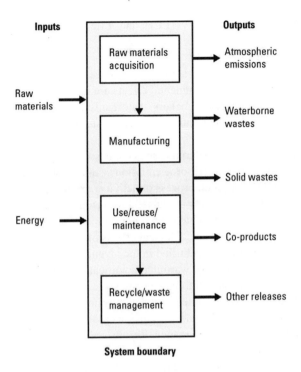

Inputs

Raw materials

Energy

Outputs

Raw materials acquisition → Atmospheric emissions

Manufacturing → Waterborne wastes

→ Solid wastes

Use/reuse/ maintenance → Co-products

Recycle/waste management → Other releases

System boundary

FIGURE 5 Life cycle stages

Source: Adapted from US Environmental Protection Agency (cited in Scientific Applications International Corporation 2006, p. 1).

Life Cycle Assessment extends beyond the boundaries of traditional product analysis, which limits consideration of the product's environmental impacts to the firm's own production processes. Life Cycle Assessment considers the impacts associated with all phases of the product, including use, re-use and disposal. Life Cycle Assessment thus requires a firm at any one point in the chain to accept responsibility for considering all these impacts in the firm's commercial decision making, whether or not that firm is itself responsible for generating these impacts. In practical terms, this means that firms will look to construct a value chain that minimises environmental impacts, while maintaining the financial viability of the firm itself. Modern practice would extend LCA to include social impacts. Clearly, this is a critical step towards handling externalities.

Life Cycle Assessment has developed over past decades. A precursor was an internal study for The Coca-Cola Company in 1969, which attempted to determine which beverage containers had the lowest releases to the environment: raw materials, fuels used and environmental loadings associated with manufacturing processes were assessed. Studies such as this led in the 1970s to the Resource and Environmental Profile Analysis (REPA) in the United States, and the Ecobalance framework in Europe. Despite some improvements in methodology, there was a reduced emphasis on LCA during the 1980s. In 1991, however, concerns expressed by a number of states in the United States about marketing claims based on LCA led to the standardisation of the LCA methodology in the ISO 14000 series. The United Nations Environment Programme (UNEP) promotes LCA methodologies through

Life Cycle Management (LCM), Life Cycle Inventory (LCI) and Life Cycle Impact Assessment (LCIA) programs.

The LCA process moves through four generic phases:

1. *Goal Definition and Scoping.* The product, process or activity to be assessed is described and defined, and the boundaries and environmental effects are identified. The nature of the information required to inform decision makers, the organisation and display of the data, the scope of the study, and the ground rules for the study are considered.

2. *Inventory Analysis (LCI).* The energy, water and materials use and environmental releases, in the form of atmospheric emissions, waterborne emissions, solid wastes, and other releases for the entire life cycle of the product, process or activity, are identified and quantified. A flow diagram of the processes being evaluated is developed; a data collection plan is established; data is collected, evaluated and reported.

3. *Impact Assessment (LCIA).* The potential human and ecological effects of energy, water and material usage and the environmental releases identified in the inventory analysis are assessed. Impact categories are developed (global warming, acidification, toxicity and so on). Inventory Analysis impacts are classified to impact categories (e.g. acid sulphate soils to acidification). Impacts are characterised, using conversion factors (e.g. from acidification factors to acid sulphate soil loads). Indicators are then normalised, grouped or ranked, and weighted for importance. Results are evaluated and reported.

4. *Interpretation.* On the basis of the inventory analysis and impact assessment, the preferred product, process or service is selected. The most significant LCA issues are identified. The completeness, sensitivity and consistency of the process are evaluated. Conclusions are reported and recommendations made. Under best-practice conditions, the LCA is subjected to peer review.

Rebitzer et al. (2004) identify a number of important financial benefits for firms utilising LCA approaches. These include reduced operating costs, from increased supply chain coordination and reduced overheads; reduced disposal costs; improved relations with authorities and agencies; improved credit terms with financial institutions; and increased revenues, from the use of reconfigured wastes and unused raw materials.

The public policy applications of LCA are also important in assessing the human and environmental effects of material consumption and environmental releases on local communities, cities and regions, including those of global significance (Scientific Applications International Corporation 2006, p. 3).

Rebitzer et al. also note the availability of public database LCI initiatives, such as the Swedish SPINE, that cover commonly used goods and services. The United States, Canada, Germany, Italy and Switzerland have also established such initiatives. Many industry sectors, such as The Association of Plastics Manufacturers in Europe (APME) and the European Aluminium Association, are developing LCA datasets. LCA software is widely available: as generic software for researchers and consultants, specialised software for specific industries or decision makers, and specialised software as an interface to business management software (p. 708).

Case study 7

Life Cycle Assessment: Nokia

The world's largest mobile phone company may not intuitively seem to be the most likely candidate for a strong environmental and social sustainability program. Nokia's commitment to sustainability initiatives can be explained in part by the Finnish corporate culture in which it is embedded (Panapanaan et al. 2003). In Finland sustainability is driven by regulatory bodies, industrial federations and employees. Finland has consistently ranked among the world's most competitive economies over the past several years in researched rankings.

The core of Nokia's sustainability program is a life cycle framework, which considers the major environmental impacts of waste and use of hazardous materials, water and energy in each phase of product development and use: raw materials, component manufacturing, own operations, logistics, use and end-of-life practices (Nokia 2010). Nokia's key environmental goals are risk management, strengthened financial performance and stakeholder acceptance.

To this life cycle framework Nokia applies the seven principles of eco-efficiency, as defined by the World Business Council for Sustainable Development:
1. minimising energy intensity
2. minimising the material intensity of goods and services
3. extension of product durability
4. increasing the efficiency of processes
5. minimising toxic dispersion
6. promoting recycling
7. maximising the use of renewable resources.

Nokia engages its major stakeholders in sustainability initiatives. It provides its employees with environmental training and competence development. It seeks input on environmental issues from consumers and corporate customers, as well as from suppliers and investors.

Legislation in Europe and elsewhere mandates systematic substance management. This requirement is managed by Nokia throughout the supplier network. Compliance is regularly monitored, and suppliers are required to have a sound EMS in place. The Nokia Substance List defines those substances that Nokia has banned, restricted or targeted for reduction. The recyclability of Nokia mobile devices ranges from 65–80 per cent.

In the context of life cycle management, Nokia has worked to reduce packaging and to utilise eco-efficient transportation. For some years the company has offered a take-back service of its mobile phones and accessories. Phone batteries are targeted for closed-loop recirculation, primarily to recover and re-use cobalt, a relatively rare and potentially hazardous metal.

Nokia measures its environmental performance on a range of indicators, including energy, gas and oil consumption; direct and indirect carbon dioxide emissions; water consumptions and discharge; and generation of waste — all recorded across the Americas, Asia–Pacific and Europea–Africa regions. Most measures show progress over the past five years.

Nokia holds its international suppliers to high standards of ethical practice. These are based on international labour standards in the International Labour Organization conventions. Basic standards are set for child and forced labour; health and safety; work associations; discrimination; disciplinary practices; working hours and remuneration. Nokia conducts regular labour assessments on its suppliers' sites. Visits have been piloted in supplier factories in China. A factory site tour is supplemented by interviews with relevant management and with workers, and a review of relevant documentation, such as payroll records. Interviews with workers are conducted in the native language by native interviewers. Corrective actions are developed in collaboration with the suppliers, and are monitored to ensure that they are carried out.

Learning objective 8 in review

8.1 The ISO approach to setting standards requires firms to measure their performance against their own stated goals and objectives. Does this guarantee better sustainability outcomes? If not, why use it?

8.2 Outline the life cycle structure of a consumer good you use every day, such as a mobile phone, computer, food or clothing item, or vehicle. Develop one sustainability measure for each stage of the life cycle you have identified.

The sustainable organisation

Attention now turns to the entity within which these sustainable business principles are carried out in practice: the organisation. Here the focus is predominantly internal, and on the human character of the business in practice. The question addressed is: What implications do sustainability principles have for the way in which the firm carries out its responsibilities to its stakeholders, particularly its own employees?

Corporate governance

A first consideration is how a company governs itself. The scope of governance includes the methods of corporate decision making, the ways in which stakeholders are included in the process, and their interests represented, and the transparent, ethical principles which are applied to all decision making. Stakeholders are considered to be both internal and external. However, responsibilities to the firm's own employees are primary, and under sustainability principles such responsibilities can redefine the nature of the employment relationship.

Modern approaches to sustainability in corporate governance

Societies are increasingly making firms more responsible for the sustainability elements, not just of the firm, but of the society at large. Bleischwitz (2007) notes that the environmental regulation initiatives of the 1970s and 1980s, with their control and command focus, have been replaced by a wider context of responsibility:

> . . . contemporary environmental policy is characterised by a shift from governments to governance, meaning that institutions and actors outside the state become more important. It is claimed not only that the acceptance of those actors is pivotal for any implementation of policies, but also that corporate and societal actors play a role in policy formulation and precautionary measures. (pp. 3–4)

The development of environmentally sustainable policy and practice is therefore seen as a collaboration of both private and public institutions.

The broad stakeholder dimension of modern corporate governance of sustainability is analysed by Kuhndt and Tunçer (2007). They see the domain of corporate governance as just such a collaboration:

> In the current state of the world, where dependency and complexity are major factors, managing sustainability problems faced at both the global and the regional level requires shared responsibilities. Among all societal actors, corporations face extended responsibilities, as they are major constructors of global product chains and contributors to global environmental and social concerns. (pp. 9–10)

Kuhndt and Tunçer develop the concept of Responsible Corporate Governance (RCG) to embody this perspective. It is framed by what they term two 'pillars'. The first consists of four elements (pp. 13–14):

1. *Stakeholder-empowered corporate governance* — through a range of involvement structures, such as those outlined in the GRI Guidelines that follow.
2. *Management and performance evaluation systems* — such as ISO 14001 (previously discussed) and SA 8000 (discussed shortly).
3. *Transparency enhancement* — through information disclosure instruments.
4. *Stakeholder verification* — for example, through accountability audits.

The second pillar relates to the establishment of the institutional framework through which stakeholders are to drive corporate accountability. This, it is proposed, is to be achieved by addressing the four elements across the stakeholder spectrum:

> A variety of actors ranging from public institutions, intergovernmental organizations, financial institutions, non-governmental organizations and research institutions to private customers can take place in a policy network with the aim of enhancing the practice of these elements by the corporation. (p. 15)

The matrix of private and public institutions is the arena of modern corporate governance. Limiting governance to the traditional boundaries of the firm cannot provide conditions for the society to address the global sustainability challenges of which it is irreversibly a part.

Governance in the Global Reporting Initiative

The Global Reporting Initiative (GRI) deals in detail with matters of corporate governance in its *G3 Guidelines* (GRI 2010). The Guidelines first require firms to describe their governance arrangements, beginning with the Board and its committees, with particular reference to those that are directly responsible for economic, social and environmental performance. The Guidelines ask for 'the mechanisms for shareholders and employees to provide recommendations or direction to the highest governance body'. With respect to employees, informing and consulting, working with formal representative bodies such as works councils, and representation of employees on the Board itself are specified. The rights of minority shareholders are emphasised.

Reporting requirements must include a link between the compensation and the organisation's performance, specifically including social and environmental performance: the Guidelines seek to hold the leaders of the organisational directly accountable for the organisation's sustainability performance.

The Guidelines further require the organisation's mission and values statements, codes of conduct and so on developed internally to embody principles relating to economic, environmental and social performance.

Reporting is also required on the external charters and guidelines relating to the sustainability factors to which the organisation subscribes, and on relevant association membership or formal links. Importantly, the Guidelines also require reporting on how the Precautionary Principle is addressed by the organisation. Finally, the governance guidelines require comprehensive reporting on stakeholder engagement.

Social accountability standards: SA 8000

Increasingly Boards, CEOs and executive teams are looking to certified standards to demonstrate their commitment to sustainable business. On the social dimensions, one such standard is SA 8000 (Social Accountability International 2001). The normative framework of SA 8000 includes an array of International Labour Organization conventions, as well as the *Universal Declaration of Human Rights*, the UN *Convention on the Rights of the Child*, and the UN *Convention to Eliminate All Forms of Discrimination Against Women*.

On the foundation of this comprehensive international framework, detailed performance and action criteria are developed for child labour, forced labour, health and safety, freedom of association and the right to collective bargaining, discrimination, disciplinary practices, working hours and remuneration. The largest category is that of management systems, which includes the development of social accountability policy and review procedures; internal communication on matters concerning the standard; planning and implementation (definition of roles, responsibilities and authority, training and awareness and monitoring); evaluation of social accountability performance of suppliers and subcontractors; corrective action; and communication, access and records. Certification is only available for a specific production facility and not for an entire group or supply chain. Certification is undertaken by external auditing bodies.

Ethical practice in governance: rules and principles

Governance in sustainable business is centrally ethical governance. Francis (2000) distinguishes between three kinds of ethical principles in governance:
1. *First-level principles*, such as equitability, which represent the highest level of aspirational standards and act as a first point of reference.
2. *Second-level principles*, such as the avoidance of conflict of interest in commercial decisions, which are implied by first-level principles when applied to commercial practice.
3. *Procedural principles*, such as making transparent allegations of ethical impropriety, which ensure stated ethical ends are achieved.

The GRI and SA 8000 frameworks are derived mainly from the last two categories. The focus here will therefore be on the first-level principles. Francis outlines seven first-level principles, which he emphasises are neither definitive nor prescriptive, but rather are a working set (pp. 116–29):
1. *Dignity*: the Kantian principle of treating each individual as an end rather than as a means to an end. This extends not only to employees but to all stakeholders.
2. *Equitability*: equitable dealing, particularly in relationships. This applies particularly to situations of unequal power.

3. *Prudence*: judgement that makes the situation no worse, and should improve the situation. It is associated with the principle of avoidance of harm, and the Precautionary Principle.
4. *Honesty*: straightforward dealing, openness, integrity and consistency.
5. *Openness*: not concealing what should be revealed or representing things as other than they are.
6. *Goodwill*: arises from concern for others and for the greater good, and from the perception of that concern in others.
7. *Suffering*: in general, pain and suffering should be prevented and alleviated.

It is rarely the case that the application of any one principle will be sufficient to resolve any issue of ethical governance. Principles frequently conflict and rank differently according to the situational context.

Francis proposes the following useful precepts in working through most ethical issues of corporate governance (2000, p. 129):

> Preserve from harm.
>
> Respect the dignity of all persons.
>
> Be open and honest except in the exceptional cases where privacy and silence are clearly ethically preferable.
>
> Act so as to preserve the equitability of relationships.

It has been argued that the framework of common morality, based in moral intuition, can be a coherent base for the application of these principles in practice, provided Boards and others responsible for ethical governance are prepared to work systematically through the issues. This is not to argue against frameworks such as the GRI Guidelines or SA 8000. Rather, it is to recognise that these frameworks are best used under general principles of ethics. In addition, as the practice of corporate governance advances under these principles and tests the limits of such frameworks, those frameworks themselves must be open to development to incorporate the new dimensions that practice indicates.

Organisational change: developing the sustainable firm

It is evident from the description of sustainable business outlined so far that in adopting sustainability principles, most firms must find new ways of doing business, often across the whole organisation. Change principles thus become central to sustainable business. The principles of change are well established in the business discipline of organisational behaviour. However, these principles take on new dimensions when considered from sustainability perspectives.

Incremental change

Dunphy, Griffiths and Benn (2003, ch. 7) distinguish four phases in the transition of an organisation from the base level, compliance, to the most developed level:
1. *From non-responsiveness to compliance.* Non-responsive organisations are those who disregard the impact of their actions on the environment, or on local communities with which they interact, or on their own people. The impetus for such organisations to

change is likely to come from sources external to the organisation, such as media exposure, public protests or court action.

2. *From compliance to sustainable efficiency.* Efficiency gains are likely to come from poorly performing units, pilot projects and capability improvement. Identification of leverage points and sharing of success are central.

3. *From efficiency to strategic proactivity.* Strategic proactivity relates to the extension of sustainability practice to products, and to suppliers and customers; to recruitment and internal development that enhances sustainability capabilities; and to active engagement with community groups in the development of new products and services.

4. *From strategic proactivity to the sustaining corporation.* The 'sustaining' corporation is characterised by a shift in the values and behaviours of the corporation, collectively and individually, towards the role of business in creating a sustainable society. There is an interaction with other organisations within the sector, or in the supply chain, to promote the implementation of sustainability practice.

The authors note that incremental change has important benefits, such as internal capability development, positive culture change and competence in the change process itself.

Transformational change

There is a well-established view, however, that a truly sustainable organisation can only be built through transformational change, since 'the operations of current businesses are so inimical to sustainability that only radical change will create a sustainable world' (p. 208). Quinn (cited in Dunphy, Griffiths & Benn 2003, p. 236) describes the kind of 'deep' change that is associated with transformational change:

> Deep change differs from incremental change in that it requires new ways of thinking and behaving. It is change that is major in scope, discontinuous with the past and generally irreversible. The deep change effort distorts existing patterns of action and involves taking risks. Deep change means surrendering control.

This is effectively reinventing the organisation. Ten steps are said to be characteristic of it (pp. 237–61):

1. *Know where you are now.* Historical analysis, surveys, interviews, focus groups and analysis of organisational records are likely to be important. Core values and perceptions, both espoused and enacted, are central.

2. *Develop the vision*: Transformational change is driven by vision. This is a creative and imaginative step: it is intended

> ... to unleash the imagination of organizational members and stakeholders so that they collaborate in creating a vision that breaks out of existing cultural assumptions to create a prototype for a truly sustainable and sustaining organization. (p. 243)

There is substantial literature on the principles and practice of vision statements (Palmer, Dunford & Akin 1991, ch. 9). The process of creating visions can be as important as the vision itself. Visions entrain systematic action.

3. *Identify the gap*: a realistic assessment is made of the gap between the present situation of the organisation and the future situation envisaged in the visioning process.

4. *Assess the readiness for change*: If the process has been conducted well to this point, commitment to change in the organisation will be building. Dunphy, Griffiths & Benn argue (pp. 247–8) that a reasoned case for change must be made and emotional commitment developed.

5. *Set the scene for action*: An intellectual momentum for change can be assisted by external agents, through exposure to sustainability experts in lectures, seminars, site visits and so on. Potential change leaders are identified and adequate resources are made available.
6. *Secure basic compliance first*: Compliance with legal requirements and the legitimate expectations of shareholders must be secured, together with a robust control system, such as ISO 14001.
7. *Move beyond compliance*: Move the organisation to strategic proactivity and the sustaining corporation by a rapid progress through the earlier steps. Risk identification and management must be in place, together with corrective responses.
8. *Establish the performance criteria for 'compliance plus'*: Output and process criteria are established to ensure that the path of organisational development tracks the transformation plan.
9. *Launch and manage the transformational change program*: Standard implementation tactics include project planning and management, communications structures, creating early wins and codifying new intellectual capital.
10. *Maintain the momentum*: Ensure that the organisation continues to monitor and respond to its level of achievement as a sustainable organisation, and to respond to changes in the external environment.

The processual approach to organisational change for sustainable business

The **processual approach** to human resource management and change is perhaps particularly well placed to drive the change sequences outlined. Processual human resource management places the focus on the individuals that constitute the organisation, particularly on their actions and interactions, in both structuring the change process and determining its outcomes. The processual approach holds that the individuals in an organisation are creative centres of action in their own right. It emphasises the primacy of individuals and of their interactions in constructing the organisation's activities and outcomes. It places attention on the two-way, interpersonal processes of interaction, negotiation and collaboration. It demands the inclusion of extra-rational processes, such as intuition and emotional engagement, in organisational decision making, alongside the familiar processes of logic and rational decision making. It accepts that organisational directions are likely to be fluid and dynamic, both internally and in response to the external environment. It sees the larger patterns of strategy as far more likely emerge from this higher-order organisational dynamic than developed at the top and cascaded down. It emphasis iterative processes and learning, and embraces 'high-commitment' approaches to the management of people, which include shared values, flat hierarchies, decentralisation, participation, devolved responsibility and ownership, enriched jobs, self-controls and continuous learning (Watson 2005).

From a sustainable business change perspective, processual approaches may well place the change manager not in the role of a director, or even a facilitator or coach, but in the role of an interpreter (Weick 2000). Four drivers are central:

1. *animation* — people remaining in motion and experimenting
2. *direction* — implementing strategies in novel ways

3. *paying attention and updating* — updating knowledge of the business environment, reviewing and reconfiguring organisational requirements
4. *respectful, candid interaction* — people being encouraged to speak out, particularly when things are not working well.

Under this model, change managers assist in interpreting how and why emerging changes are occurring, both 'to make sense of events that don't fit together' and to 'certify change'. This may also include a role based on the ethics of care, where change managers 'may nurture their organizations, facilitating organizational qualities that enable positive self-organizing to occur' (Palmer, Dunford & Akin 1991, pp. 31–3).

This approach indicates the value of 'practical wisdom' in approaching the decision to change in ethical and sustainable directions. This Aristotelian concept (Aristotle, trans. Ross 1925) suggests that ethical decision making is 'not the rationally instrumental production of previously-identified, normatively positive outcomes, but instead a performative enactment of the common good'.

Above all, the ethical core of sustainable business requires the cultivation of balance, a central quality of what is described as wisdom:

> Wisdom is not simply about maximizing one's own or someone else's self-interest, but about balancing of various self-interests (intrapersonal) with the interests of others (interpersonal) and of other aspects of the context in which one lives (extrapersonal) . . . (Sternberg, cited in Statler & Oppengaard 2007, p. 176)

This is regarded not as a means to an end but as a valued end in itself — the core of what it means for an enterprise to be sustainable. Balance on this level emerges only in practice: it is wise practice that builds and integrates ethics and effectiveness. For the firm, the outcome is not only sustained profitability, but consistently 'acting well'.

Learning objective 9 in review

9.1 Sustainability principles are often seen as applying mainly to impacts outside the firm. What justifies their application inside the firm?

9.2 Do you agree with the common assertion that the change to a sustainable firm is best driven from the top?

Glossary

Assets Probable future economic benefits obtained or controlled by a particular entity as a result of past transactions. In sustainable accounting, assets may be defined to include the natural capital upon which a reporting entity is economically dependent. *p. 34*

Best Available Technology Economically Achievable (BTEA) The best technology for pollution control currently in use or commercially available. *p. 50*

Best Practice Environmental Management (BPEM) Environmental management of an activity which achieves ongoing minimisation of environmental harm through cost-effective measures assessed against measures currently used nationally and internationally for that activity. *p. 50*

Cost allocation Indirect costs not traceable to particular products or departments are allocated to, or identified with, those objectives. *p. 37*

Discounted cash flow (DCF) valuation In DCF valuation, the value of an asset is the present value of the expected cash flows on the asset, discounted back at a rate that reflects the riskiness of these cash flows. *p. 38*

Environmental Management Accounting (EMA) Includes Triple Bottom Line (TBL) reporting, corporate social responsibility, environmental management systems (EMS), environmental cost accounting, product and production decision making, supply chain management, International Organization for Standardization (ISO) standards, the balanced scorecard and environmentally oriented capital expenditure analysis. *p. 36*

Environmental Management System (EMS) A corporate system for pollution prevention that informs management and employees at all levels of an organisation how to approach their pollution prevention responsibilities. *p. 50*

Ethical practice Ethical principles are applied to entire fields, such as medical ethics and business ethics, and to particular issues, such as affirmative action, labour rights and natural resource management. *p. 20*

Ethics A major branch of philosophy about thinking and acting rightly or wrongly. Descriptive ethics describes the ethical systems of a society, culture or group of people. Normative ethics seeks to show how people ought to act. *p. 20*

Expenses Outflows or other using up of assets (in sustainable accounting, including the consumption of natural capital) or the incurrence of liabilities (or a combination of both) from delivering or producing goods, rendering services, or carrying out other activities that constitute the entity's ongoing major or central operations (in sustainable accounting, including the preventive maintenance of the natural capital essential to maintain a going concern). *p. 34*

Externalities The costs and benefits that are associated with transactions, but which accrue to others, and which are therefore not taken into account when the market actors make their decisions. *p. 28*

Free cash flows to the firm (FCFF) Cash flows from assets, before debt payments but after the firm has reinvested to create growth assets. *p. 38*

Gross domestic product (GDP) The output produced by factors of production located in the domestic economy. *p. 11*

Gross national product (GNP) Total income earned by domestic citizens regardless of the country in which their factor services were supplied. GNP thus equals GDP plus net property income from abroad. *p. 11*

Liabilities Liabilities arise from present obligations or a particular entity to transfer assets or provide services to other entities in the future, as a result of past transactions or events. Sustainable accounting may include, in this definition, the risk of the consumption of natural capital. *p. 34*

Market A market is composed of demanders and suppliers, who are real human beings pursuing the projects that interest them, economising on the basis of the relative scarcities that they confront and negotiating arrangements to secure what they want from others by offering others what they, in turn, want to obtain. *p. 28*

Market failure Market failure is a term used to describe situations where markets are unable to form, or, having formed, are unable to capture all the relevant costs and benefits. *p. 28*

National Environment Protection Measures (NEPM) National standards, goals, guidelines or protocols made with respect to specific areas, such as ambient air and water quality, re-use and recycling, motor vehicle noise and emissions, and guidelines for assessment of site contamination. *pp. 49–50*

Neoclassical economics The neoclassical framework centres on economics agents, such as households or firms, making decisions to maximise their net economic benefits under constraints. These decisions are worked out in markets through price signals. *p. 11*

Overheads Overheads are indirect material, labour and other costs which are not specifically identified with the cost objective. They can be fixed costs, such as insurance or rates, or variable costs, such as power. *p. 37*

Private costs Costs which are incurred and paid for by a firm in producing a good or service. *p. 29*

Processual approach Emphasises the primacy of individuals and of their interactions in constructing the organisation's activities and outcomes. It places attention on the two-way, interpersonal processes of interaction, negotiation and collaboration. *p. 61*

Real Options Options for which there is a right, without obligation, of a real, rather than a financial, nature. *p. 40*

Reporting entity The entity assumption treats a firm or organisation as an accounting unit. It follows that transactions are only recorded if they affect the accounting unit. Factors and impact external to the accounting entity will be ignored. *p. 33*

Rights theory Rights are natural rights that constitute human dignity: they are inalienable or entitlement claims which all individuals have, regardless of their membership in any state or social organisation. *p. 21*

Social costs All the costs of production of some resource-related good or service, including costs which are incurred by the firm's use of commonly owned resources but not paid for by the firm. *p. 29*

Social marketing The application of commercial marketing technologies to the analysis, planning, execution and evaluation of programs designed to influence the voluntary or involuntary behaviour of target audiences in order to improve the welfare of individuals and society. *p. 45*

Stakeholder theory Asserts the legitimacy of claims on the firm by a number of other constituencies, whose interests may vary widely. A stakeholder is an individual or a group which either is harmed by, or benefits from, the corporation; or whose rights can be violated, or have to be respected, by the corporation. *p. 19*

Strong sustainability Strong sustainability accepts that elements of natural resource inputs have historically been offset by the application of physical, human and intellectual capital, but argues that there are important elements of natural capital that cannot be substituted for by human capital.   *p. 11*

Sustainability Sustainability has become a term of wide currency, yet its definition and scope is far from agreed. It is often linked to 'sustainable development'. Current usage (drawn from the Rio Declaration on Environment and Development) embraces economic, environmental and social dimensions. With respect to the firm, some include governance. In systems terminology, sustainability has been related to the maintenance of the stock of natural and social capital over time. *p. 4*

Sustainability marketing Marketing which is governed by sustainability principles and objectives, across environmental, social and economic dimensions.   *p. 44*

Sustainable accounting Attempts to configure the conceptual framework of financial accounting so as to bring sustainability factors into accounting practice.   *p. 34*

Sustainable business Sustainable business can be trivially interpreted to mean continuously profitable business. In this book, sustainable business is the business of firms under sustainability principles.   *p. 4*

Sustainable development According to the UN World Commission on Environment and Development, sustainable development 'seeks to meet the needs and aspirations of the present without compromising the ability to meet those of the future'.   *p. 7*

Utilitarian theory An ethical framework which holds that the moral worth of actions is to be found not in the nature of the actions themselves, but in their consequences. It holds that a society should seek always to produce the maximum amount of good, and the least amount of harm, for all those persons. *p. 20*

Value In DCF valuation, the value of the asset is the aggregated present values of the cash flows the asset is projected to generate.   *p. 39*

Weak sustainability Weak sustainability holds that there is a high degree of substitutability between human and intellectual capital and natural capital. Proponents of this view argue for a concept of sustainability in which the sum of human and natural capital is non-declining.   *p. 10*

References

Alberti, M, Caini, L, Calabrese, A & Rossi, D 2000, 'Evaluation of the costs and benefits of an environmental management system', *International Journal of Production Research*, vol. 38, no. 17, pp. 4455–66.

Aristotle 1925, *The Nicomachean ethics*, trans. D. Ross, Oxford University Press, Oxford.

Australian Building Codes Board 2008, *The Building Code of Australia*, www.abcb.gov.au.

Australian Petroleum Production & Exploration Association 1996, *Code of environmental practice*, www.appea.com.au.

Babe, R 2006, *Culture of ecology: reconciling economics and environment*, University of Toronto Press, Toronto.

Bates, G 2006, *Environmental law in Australia*, 6th edn, Reed International Books, Australia.

Beauchamp, T & Bowie, N 2004, *Ethical theory and business*, 7th edn, Pearson Prentice Hall, New Jersey.

Belz, F & Peattie, K 2009, *Sustainability marketing: a global perspective*, John Wiley & Sons, Chichester, United Kingdom.

Berle, A & Means, G 1932, *The modern corporation and private property*, revised edition 1967, Harcourt, Brace and World Inc, New York.

Bleischwitz, R 2007 'Scope and main thesis' in *Corporate governance of sustainability: a co-evolutionary view on resource management*, ed. R Bleischwitz, Edward Elgar, Cheltenham, UK, pp. 3–7.

Bowie, N 2002, 'A Kantian approach to business ethics' in *Ethical issues in business: a philosophical approach*, eds. T Donaldson, P Werhane & M Cording, Pearson Education, New Jersey.

Carson, R 1965, *Silent spring*, Penguin Books, Middlesex.

Carson, R, Mitchell, R, Hanemann, M, Kopp, R, Presser, S & Ruud, P 2004, 'Contingent valuation and loss passive use: damages from the Exxon Valdez oil spill', *Environmental and Resource Economics*, vol. 25, no. 3, pp. 257–86.

Cassidy, J 2003, *Concise corporations law*, 4th edn, The Federation Press, Leichardt, NSW.

Clegg, B 2009, *Eco-logic: cutting through the greenwash: truth, lies and saving the planet*, Eden Project, London.

Coase, R 1937, 'The nature of the firm', *Economica*, vol.4xxx, reprinted in R Coase 1988, *The firm, the market and the law*, The University of Chicago Press, Chicago, pp. 33–55.

Coase, R 1960, 'The problem of social cost', *The Journal of Law and Economics*, vol. 3, pp. 1–44, reprinted in R Coase 1988, *The firm, the market and the law*, The University of Chicago Press, Chicago, pp. 95–166.

Common, M 1995, *Sustainability and policy: limits to economics*, Cambridge University Press, Melbourne.

Common, M & Perrings, S 1992, 'Towards an ecological economics of sustainability', *Ecological Economics*, vol. 6, no. 1, pp. 7–34.

Common, M & Stagl, S 2005 *Ecological economics*, Cambridge University Press, Cambridge.

Crane, A & Matten, D 2007 *Business ethics*, 2nd edn, Oxford University Press, Oxford.

Crowe, R & Williams, S 2001, *Who are the ethical consumers?* Co-operative Bank, London.

Daly, H 1991, *Steady-state economics*, 2nd edn, Island Press, Washington DC.

Daly, H 1997, *Beyond growth: the economics of sustainable development*, Beacon Press, Boston MA.

Daly, H & Cobb, J 1994, *For the common good: redirecting the economy toward community, the environment, and sustainable future*, Beacon Press, Boston MA.

Daly, H & Farley, J 2001, *Ecological economics: principles and applications*, 2nd edn, Island Press, Washington DC.

Damodaran, A 2006, *Damodaran on valuation: security analysis for investment and corporate finance*, 2nd edn, John Wiley & Sons, New Jersey.

Davis, J & Devinney, T 1997, *The essence of corporate strategy: theory for modern decision making*, Allen & Unwin, St Leonards, Australia.

Deegan, C 2009, *Financial accounting theory*, 3rd edn, McGraw-Hill Education, New York.

Donovan, RJ & Henley, N 2003, *Social marketing: principles and practice*. Melbourne: IP Communications.

Dow Jones Indexes, Stoxx Ltd & SAM Group 2010, Dow Jones Sustainability World Components, www.sustainability-indexes.com.

Drucker, P 1946, *The concept of the corporation*, reprinted 1993, Transaction Publishers, Rutgers University, New Jersey.

Drucker, P 1968, *Managing for results*, HarperCollins Publishers, New York.

Dunphy, D, Griffiths, A & Benn, S 2003, *Organizational change for corporate sustainability*, Routledge, London.

Eckersley, R 2004, *Well & good: how we feel and why it matters*, Text Publishing, Melbourne.

Elkington, J 1999, *Cannibals with forks: the triple bottom line of 21st century business*, Capstone Publishing Ltd, Oxford, UK.

Empowerment Institute 2004, *Sustainable lifestyle campaign*, Woodstock, New York: Empowerment Institute.

Erlich, P 1968, *The population bomb*, Ballantine Books, New York.

European Convention 2000, 'Charter of fundamental rights of the European Union', *Official Journal of the European Communities*, C 364, 18 December, www.europarl.europa.eu.

Field, B 2008, *Natural resource economics: an introduction*, 2nd edn, Irwin/McGraw-Hill, New York.

Field, B & Field, M 2005, *Environmental economics: an introduction*, Irwin/McGraw-Hill, New York.

Figge, F 2005, 'Value-based environmental management: from environmental shareholder value to environmental option value', *Corporate Social Responsibility and Environmental Management*, vol. 12, pp. 19–30.

Fisher, D 2003, *Australian environmental law*, Lawbook Co., Pyrmont NSW.

Foster, J (ed.) 1997, *Valuing nature? Ethics, economics and the environment*, Routledge, London.

Francis, R 2000, *Ethics and corporate governance: an Australian handbook*, University of New South Wales Press, Sydney.

Freeman, R 1984, *Strategic management: a stakeholder approach*, Pitman, Boston.

Friedman, M 1970, 'The social responsibility of business is to increase its profits', *The New York Times Magazine*, 13 September 1970, The New York Times Company, New York.

Global Action Plan 1995, *America puts its house in order, household by household* Woodstock, New York: Global Action Plan for the Earth.

Global Reporting Initiative 2010, *Sustainability reporting guidelines: G3 Guidelines*, Amsterdam, The Netherlands.

Gray, R & Bebbington, J 2001, *Accounting for the environment*, Sage Publications, Thousand Oaks, California.

Gray, R, Owen, D & Adams, C 1996, *Accounting and accountability: changes and challenges in corporate social and environmental reporting*, Prentice Hall, London.

GRI — *see* Global Reporting Initiative.

Habermas, J 1990, *Moral consciousness and communicative action*, Polity Press, Cambridge, UK.

Hamilton, C 2003 *The growth fetish*, Allen & Unwin, Crows Nest.

Hanson, D & Stuart, H 2001, 'Failing the reputation management test: the case of BHP, the Big Australian', *Corporate Reputation Review*, vol. 4, no. 2, pp. 128–43.

Hardin, G 1968, 'The tragedy of the commons', *Science*, 13 December 1968.

Harland, P 1995, *The effectiveness of the EcoTeam program in the Netherlands*. Leiden, Netherlands: Department of Social and Organizational Psychology, University of Leiden.

Hawken, P 1993, *The ecology of commerce: how business can save the planet*, Weidenfeld and Nicolson, London.

Hawken, P & Lovins, L 1999, *Natural capitalism: creating the next industrial revolution*, Little, Brown and Co., Boston.

Henderson, S, Peirson, G & Harris, K 2004, *Financial accounting theory*, Pearson Education Australia, Frenchs Forest, NSW.

Heyne, P, Boettke, P & Prychitko, D 2003, *The economic way of thinking*, 10th edn, Prentice Hall, Upper Saddle River, New Jersey.

IASB — *see* International Accounting Standards Board.

ICAA — *see* Institute of Chartered Accountants in Australia.

Institute of Chartered Accountants in Australia (ICAA) 2003, *Environmental management accounting: an introduction and case studies for Australia*, Melbourne.

Institute of Chartered Accountants in England and Wales (ICAEW) 1975, *The Corporate Report*, Accounting Standards Steering Committee, Institute of Chartered Accountants in England and Wales, London.

International Accounting Standards Board (IASB) 2007, *IASB agenda project: conceptual framework*, London, www.iasplus.com.

International Panel on Climate Change 2010, *The IPCC assessment reports*, www.ipcc.ch.

IPCC — *see* International Panel on Climate Change.

Irwin, E & Clark, J 2006, *The local costs and benefits of Wal-Mart*, Department of Agricultural, Environmental and Development Economics, The Ohio State University.

Issaquah EcoTeam 1998, *Program survey*. Woodstock, New York: Global Action Plan for the Earth.

Jacobs, M 1991, *The green economy*, Pluto Press, UK.

Kagan, S 1998, *Normative ethics*, Westview Press, Oxford.

Kassirer, J & McKenzie-Mohr, D 1998, *Tools of change: Proven Methods for Promoting Environmental Citizenship*. Ottawa, Ontario, Canada: National Round Table on the Environment and the Economy.

Kneese, A & Schulze, W 1985, 'Ethics and environmental economics' in *Handbook of natural resource and energy economics*, vol. 1, ch. 5, (eds) A Kneese & J Sweeney, Elsevier Science Publishers, Amsterdam.

Kotler, P, Roberto, N & Lee, N (2002) *Social marketing: Improving the Quality of Life*. Thousand Oaks, California: Sage Publications

Kuhndt, M & Tunçer, B 2007, 'Sustainability as a business challenge: the concept of responsible corporate governance' in *Corporate governance of sustainability: a co-evolutionary view on resource management*, (ed.) R Bleischwitz, Edward Elgar, Cheltenham, UK, pp. 8–25.

Labatt, S & White, R 2007, Carbon finance: the financial implications of climate change, Wiley & Sons, New Jersey.

Langfield-Smith, K, Thorne, H & Hilton, R 2006, *Management accounting: information for managing and creating value*, McGraw-Hill, North Ryde, NSW.

Leopold, A 1949, *A sand county almanac*, Oxford University Press, Oxford.

Lovelock, J 1989, *The ages of Gaia: a biography of our living earth*, Oxford University Press, Oxford.

Lovelock, J 2007, *The revenge of Gaia: earth's climate crisis and the fate of humanity*, Perseus Books Group, New York.

Lutz, M 1999, *Economics for the common good: two centuries of social economic thought in the humanistic tradition*, Routledge, Oxford, UK.

MacDonald, C & Whellams, M 2007, 'Corporate decisions about labelling genetically modified foods', *Journal of Business Ethics*, vol. 75, pp. 181–9.

MacGillivray, A 2000, 'The Fair Share of the growing market share of green and ethical products', *New Economics Foundation*, June, pp. 27–42.

Maitland, I 2005, 'The great non-debate over international sweatshops' in *Case studies in business ethics*, 5th edn, (ed.) A Gini, Pearson Prentice Hall, New Jersey.

Malthus, T 1798, *An essay on the principle of population*, (ed.) A Flew, Penguin Books, Harmondsworth, UK.

Marsh, G 1864, *Man and nature*, Sampson Low, Son and Marston, London.

Marshall, A 1890, *Principles of economics*, 8th edn, 1920, Macmillan, London.

Martin, J & Petty, J 2000, *Value based management*, Harvard Business School Press, Boston, MA.

McCormack, G 1996, *The emptiness of Japanese affluence*, Allen & Unwin, New York.

McKenzie-Mohr, D & Smith, W 1999, *Fostering sustainable behavior*. Gabriola Island BC Canada: New Society Publishers.

Meadows, DH, Meadows, DL, Randers, J & Behrens, W 1972, *The limits to growth: a report for the Club of Rome's project on the predicament of mankind*, Earth Island, Universe Books, New York.

Meadows, DH, Meadows, DL & Randers J 1992, *Beyond the limits to growth: global collapse or sustainable future*, Earthscan Publications Ltd, London.

Meadows, DH, Meadows, DL & Randers J 2005, *Limits to growth: the 30-year update*, Earthscan Publications Ltd, London.

Minerals Council of Australia 2005, *Enduring value: the Australian minerals industry framework for sustainable development*, www.minerals.org.au.

Mishan, E 1967 *The costs of economic growth*, Penguin Books, Middlesex.

Muir, J 1912, *The Yosemite*, The Century Co., New York.

National Research Council 2002, *The drama of the commons*, Committee on the Human Dimensions of Global Change, (eds) E Ostrum, T Dietz, N Dolsak, P Stern, S Stonich & E Weber, Division of Behavioural and Social Science and Education, National Academy Press, Washington DC.

Newburry, W & Gladwin, T 2002, 'Shell and Nigerian Oil' in *Ethical issues in business: a philosophical approach*, (eds) T Donaldson, P Werhane & M Cording, Pearson Education, New Jersey.

Nokia 2010, *The power of we: working together to protect the environment*, Nokia, Keilalahdentie, Finland, www.nokia.com.

Palmer, I, Dunford, R & Akin, G 1991, *Managing organizational change: a multiple perspectives approach*, McGraw-Hill Irwin, New York.

Panapanaan, V, Linnanen, L, Karvonen, M & Phan, V 2003, 'Roadmapping corporate social responsibility in Finnish companies', *Journal of Business Ethics*, vol. 44, no. 2–3, pp. 133–48.

Pareto, V 1906 *Manual of political economy*, trans. A Schwier, AM Kelley, New York.

Pearce, D, Markandya, A & Barbier, E 1989, *Blueprint for a green economy*, Earthscan Publications Ltd, London.

Pearce, D & Turner, R 1990, *Economics of natural resources and the environment*, Harvester Wheatsheaf, Hemel Hempstead, UK.

Peirson, G, Brown, R, Easton, S, Howard, P & Pinder, S 2009, *Business Finance*, 9th edn, McGraw-Hill Australia Pty Ltd, North Ryde, NSW.

Perman, R, Ma, Y, McGilvray, J & Common, M 2003, *Natural resource and environmental economics*, Pearson Education Ltd., Essex.

Pigou, A 1920, *The economics of welfare*, Macmillan, London.

Princen, T 2005. *The logic of sufficiency*, The MIT Press, Cambridge, MA.

Rawls, J 1972, *A theory of justice*, Oxford University Press, Oxford.

Rebitzer, G, Ekvall, T, Frischknecht, R, Hunkeler, D, Norris, G, Rydberg, T, Schmidt, WP, Suh, S, Weidma, B & Pennington, D 2004, 'Life cycle assessment: Part 1: framework, goal and scope definition, inventory analysis, and applications', *Environment International*, vol. 30, p. 701–20.

Redclift, M & Sage, C 1998, 'Global environmental change and global inequality', *International Sociology*, vol. 13, no. 4, pp. 499–516.

Rubenstein, D 1994, *Environmental accounting for the sustainable corporation: strategies and techniques*, Quorum Books, Westport CT.

Scientific Applications International Corporation (SAIC) 2006, *Life cycle assessment: principles and practice*, National Risk Management Research Laboratory, Office of Research and Development, U.S. Environmental Protection Agency, Cincinnati, Ohio.

Sen, A 1987, *On ethics and economics*, Blackwell, Oxford.

Simon, J 1981, *The ultimate resource*, Princeton University Press, Princeton, New Jersey.

Social Accountability International 2001, *Social Accountability 8000*, Social Accountability International, New York.

Staats, HJ & Harland, P 1995, *The EcoTeam Program in the Netherlands: A longitudinal study on the effects of the EcoTeam Program on environmental behaviour and its psychological backgrounds*, Amsterdam: Ministry of the Environment, Netherlands.

Statler, M & Oppengaard, K 2007, 'Practical wisdom: integrating ethics and effectiveness in organisations' in *Business ethics as practice: representation, reflexivity and* performance, (eds) C Carter, S Clegg, M Kornberger, S Laske & M Messner, Edward Elgar, Cheltenham, UK, pp. 169–89.

Stretton, H 1976, *Capitalism, socialism and the environment*, Cambridge University Press, Cambridge.

Stretton, H 2000, *Economics: a new introduction*, Pluto Press, London.

Tallontire, A 2001, *Ethical consumers and ethical trade*, Policy Series 12, Natural Resources Institute, Chatham, UK.

Tietenberg, T 1984, *Marketable emission permits in theory and practice*, paper presented at the conference, Economics of Energy and Environmental Problems, Vaxholm, Sweden.

Tietenberg, T 2000, *Environmental and natural resource economics*, HarperCollins, New York.

Tietenberg, T, 2004, *Environmental economics and policy*, Pearson Education, New Jersey.

United Nations 1948, *The Universal Declaration of Human Rights*, www.un.org/en.

UNDESA — *see* United Nations Department of Economic and Social Affairs.

UNDSD — *see* United Nations Division for Sustainable Development.

United Nations Department of Economic and Social Affairs (UNDESA) 1999, *Rio declaration on environment and development, Rio de Janeiro 1992*, United Nations, New York.

United Nations Division for Sustainable Development (UNDSD) 2001, *Environmental management accounting: procedures and principles*, United Nations, New York.

Walmart 2010, *Global Sustainability Report 2010 Progress Update*, Walmart, Bentonville, Arkansas, http://walmartstores.com.

Walmart n.d., *Diversity*, Walmart, Bentonville, Arkansas, http://walmartstores.com.

Watson, T 2005, 'Organisations, strategies and human resourcing' in *The strategic managing of human resources*, (eds) J Leopold, L Harris & T Watson, Pearson Education Limited, Harlow, Essex, pp. 6–33.

WCED — *see* World Commission on Environment and Development.

Weick, K 2000, 'Emergent change as a universal in organizations' in *Breaking the code of change*, (eds) M Beer & N Nohria, Harvard Business School Press, Boston, pp. 223–41.

Wells, G 2007, *Measuring carbon value-at-risk, value-of-gain*, Presentation to Melbourne Centre for Financial Studies, 16 May 2007, Melbourne, www.melbournecentre.com.au.

Weybrecht, G 2009, *The sustainable MBA: the manager's guide to green business*, Wiley & Sons, Chichester, United Kingdom.

Wheale, P & Hinton, D 2007, 'Ethical consumers in search of markets', *Business Strategy and the Environment*, vol. 16, no. 4, pp. 302–15.

Whitelaw, K 2004, *ISO 14001 environmental systems handbook*, 2nd edn, Elsevier/Butterworth Heinemann, Amsterdam.

Wills, I 2006, Economics and the environment: a signalling and incentives approach, 2nd edn, Allen & Unwin, Crows Nest, NSW.

World Commission on Environment and Development (WCED) 1987, *Our Common Future*, Oxford University Press, Oxford.

World Resources Institute 2008, *Earthtrends*, http://earthtrends.wri.org.

WRI — *see* World Resources Institute.

Index